Giannis Andreou is a self-made entrepreneur/investor/social influencer who possesses various skills. He started as a self-taught entrepreneur and then trained by the world's most successful millionaires and billionaires online and offline. He has over 12 years of experience in the digital economy.

★★★ Skills and Expertise ★★★

✓ Blockchain and cryptocurrencies

✓ Online and offline marketing

✓ Sales

✓ Electronic commerce

✓ Social media marketing

✓ Public speaking

✓ Real estate, personal finance and wealth creation

✓ Branding social media

✓ Affiliate marketing

Giannis has skills and knowledge not only in the digital economy, but also in interpersonal relations.

Over the last 10 years, he has taught the above topics to over 1000,000 people all over the world through his academy and social media.

He is also the author of other books and the creator of educational programs. Giannis has created over 30 online courses as well as over 4000 educational videos, most of which can be found on Giannis Andreou's social media accounts. In the last two years, he has created over 1400 free educational videos on his YouTube channel about cryptocurrencies, which are a new sector in the world of finance. Currently, his channel has reached to be the #1 channel in Greece and Cyprus for cryptocurrencies and now expanding all over the world.

Giannis has created his own online academy for the digital economy, *andreouuniversity.com*. There he has his own course series, as well as courses from other experts in cryptocurrencies, e-commerce, social media, and online marketing and much more

Scan the QR code or visit *andreouuniversity.com*

Giannis Andreou

THE ULTIMATE GUIDE TO CRYPTOCURRENCY

The Ultimate Guide for Blockchain, Cryptocurrencies, WEB 3.0, NFTs and DeFi, For Understanding

AUSTIN MACAULEY PUBLISHERS™

LONDON * CAMBRIDGE * NEW YORK * SHARJAH

Copyright © Giannis Andreou 2024

The right of Giannis Andreou to be identified as author of this work has been asserted by the author in accordance with Federal Law No. (7) of UAE, Year 2002, Concerning Copyrights and Neighboring Rights.

All rights reserved. No part of this publication may be reproduced, stored in a retrieval system, or transmitted in any form or by any means, electronic, mechanical, photocopying, recording, or otherwise, without the prior permission of the publishers.

Any person who commits any unauthorized act in relation to this publication may be liable to legal prosecution and civil claims for damages.

ISBN 9789948766742 (Paperback)
ISBN 9789948766735 (E-Book)

Application Number: MC-10-01-2467578
Age Classification: E

The age group that matches the content of the books has been classified according to the age classification system issued by the Ministry of Culture and Youth.

Printer Name: iPrint Global Ltd
Printer Address: Witchford, England

First Published 2024
AUSTIN MACAULEY PUBLISHERS FZE
Sharjah Publishing City
P.O Box [519201]
Sharjah, UAE
www.austinmacauley.ae
+971 655 95 202

I have to start by thanking my awesome family for their endless support all these years. My one million+ audience on my social media for their support and validation of my contribution, and all my mentors who are responsible for my success.

Table of Contents

Disclaimer	13
Introduction	15
Cryptocurrencies	15
Opportunities and risks	18
Blockchain – Its Relation to Cryptocurrencies	20
What Is Blockchain?	20
What Is a "Database"?	20
How Does Blockchain Work for Bitcoin?	21
Decentralization	22
Blockchain Advantages	23
Use Cases of Blockchain	23
Blockchain Disadvantages	25
Conclusion	26
The Bitcoin	27
The Beginning of Bitcoin	27
What Is Bitcoin?	28
Basic Data About BTC	28
Understanding Bitcoin	29
Bitcoin Mining	31
Historical Facts of Bitcoin	31
Who Is Satoshi Nakamoto?	32
Investing in Bitcoin	34
Types of Risks Associated with Investing in Bitcoin	34
The Risks of Investing in Crypto	35

Security Risk in Exchanges and Wallets	36
Risks Around Investing in Bitcoin	38
Scams Around the Bitcoin Issue	39
What Happens When There Are Disagreements in the Cryptocurrency Community	43

Proof of Work (PoW) and Proof of Stake (PoS) — 45

What Is Proof of Work (PoW)?	45
What Is Proof of Stake (PoS)?	47
What Is the Difference Between Proof of Work and Proof of Stake?	48

Investment Strategies — 50

Strategy 1: Value Investing	52
Strategy 2: Growth Investing	53
Strategy 3: Momentum Investing – Hype	55
Shorting	55
Strategy 4: Dollar Cost Averaging (DCA)	56
A Wise Choice	57
Once You Have Defined Your Strategy	58
The Bottom Line	59

What Is Trading? — 60

What Is Cryptocurrency Trading?	60
CFD Transactions in Cryptocurrencies	61
Buying and Selling Cryptocurrencies Through an Exchange	61
New to Cryptocurrencies	62
CoinMarketCap	62
CoinGecko	64
OKX Exchange	65
Binance Exchange	65
Trust Wallet	65
MetaMask	65
How to Buy Cryptocurrencies?	66

What Is a Cryptocurrency Broker?	*70*
What Are NFTs?	**71**
What Determines the Value of an NFT	*71*
How to Buy an NFT	*72*
NFT Buying Tips	*74*
How Do You Know What NFTs to Buy?	*75*
Finally, Why Do People Buy Digital Art on NFTs?	*75*
How to Create and Sell an NFT	*76*
What Is Minting?	*80*
Why Are NFTs so Popular?	**81**
The Popularity of NFTs	*81*
Some Good NFTs	*83*
Axie Infinity	*84*
Decentraland	*84*
CryptoPunks	*84*
Gods Unchained	*85*
The Sandbox	*85*
NBA TopShot	*85*
Bored Ape Yacht Club	*85*
Remarkable Women	*86*
Cyber Cosmos World	*86*
CryptoKitties	*86*
Bull Market and Bear Market	**87**
What Is a Bull Market?	*87*
How Does the Bull Market Work?	*87*
How Long Does It Take to End a Bull Market?	*88*
Characteristics of a Bull Market	*88*
Bull Run	*89*
Bear Trend and Bear Market	*90*

Wyckoff Investment Method — 96

The Law of Cause and Effect — 97
The Law of Supply and Demand — 97
The Law of Effort Versus Result — 98
The Best Ways to Learn Technical Analysis — 99

Cryptocurrencies and the S&P 500 Index — 103

A Comparison of Cryptocurrencies with the S&P 500 index — 103

Mistakes We Make in Investing — 107

The Number One Secret of My Success — 108

20 Top Crypto Projects — 111

Bitcoin (BTC) — 111
Ethereum (ETH) — 112
Solana (SOL) — 114
XRP Ledger (XRPL) — 116
Polygon (MATIC) — 118
Cardano (ADA) — 121
Flux (FLUX) — 122
Cosmos (ATOM) — 124
Arbitrum (ARB) — 126
Elrond (EGLD) — 128
Mina Protocol (MINA) — 131
The Sandbox (SAND) — 136
Decentraland (MANA) — 138
Helium (HNT) — 140
Hedera (HBAR) — 142
Aptos (APT) — 143
Audius (AUDIO) — 144
NEAR Protocol (NEAR) — 147
OKB (OKB) — 149

The Meme Coins and Their Function — 152
The Function of the Meme Coins — 154
Security in Meme Coins — 155
Dogecoin (DOGE) — 156
Shiba Inu (SHIB) — 157
Pepe (PEPE) — 158

Cryptocurrency Exchanges — 160
Author's Note: Evaluating Cryptocurrency Exchanges — 160
OKX Exchange — 161
Binance Exchange — 163
Some Important Events — 165

Cryptocurrencies of Binance — 166
Binance Coin (BNB) — 166

Bybit Exchange — 172

Bitget Exchange — 175

KuCoin Exchange — 178
Gate.io Exchange — 180

Platforms for Staking and Farming — 182
Platforms to Earn Interest with Your Cryptocurrency — 182

OKX — 184
Binance — 186

Bybit — 188
Bitget — 188
Nexo — 189

PancakeSwap — 192

5 AI Cryptocurrency Projects — 194
Worldcoin (WLD) — 194
The Graph (GRT) — 196

Fetch.ai (FET)	*197*
Ocean Protocol (OCEAN)	*199*
SingularityNET (AGIX)	*201*

The Future – Web 3.0/Web3 — **204**

1. Helium (HNT)	*205*
2. Chainlink (LINK)	*206*
3. Filecoin (FIL)	*206*
4. Flux (FLUX)	*206*
5. Theta (THETA)	*207*
6. The Graph (GRT)	*207*
7. BitTorrent (BTT)	*207*
8. Siacoin (SC)	*207*
9. Basic Attention Token (BAT)	*208*
10. Polkadot (DOT)	*208*

Decentralized Means of Social Networking — **209**

All.me	*210*
Mastodon.social	*210*
Minds.com	*211*
Steemit	*211*
SocialX	*211*
DLive.tv	*212*
Honest.cash	*212*
Diaspora Foundation.org	*212*
PropsProject	*213*
Sapien	*213*

Epilogue — **215**

Glossary — **218**

Bibliography – References — **239**

Disclaimer

I am not an investment advisor and I do not give investment advice in this book. The data here is all the information I have found from my research, and in some places, I express my opinion according to my understanding of it. Everyone is responsible for doing their own research and study and making responsible decisions about their investments. Of course, if necessary, they can consult a certified investment advisor.

I have been following this market since I learned about Bitcoin in 2012. I am writing this book after tens of thousands of hours of study, having over 10 years of experience and watching this market. For the last two years, it has been my main occupation as an entrepreneur, investor, influencer, analyst, educator, and content creator for cryptocurrencies. I have created over 1200 videos about cryptocurrencies and posted them on social media. In this book, I have compiled the most important information you need to know right now, which I have researched and found to be valid, according to my understanding, and so I am providing it to help you learn a few more things about this new world.

It is up to you to agree or disagree with the views or ideas presented.

This book contains links and QR codes that are referral links. If the reader makes use of these links or QR codes, then this platform will distribute a referral bonus to the user and the referrer.

GLOSSARY

At the end of this book, there is a glossary with definitions of the terms you will encounter as you read it. I suggest that you find the terms in the glossary that you do not fully understand while reading the book, and read their definitions to get a better understanding of the text and data.

Introduction

Cryptocurrencies

Cryptocurrencies and blockchain is a new and promising technology. It promises to revolutionize the global economy, both in the way we transact and in the way we hold and transfer value through "Blockchain" technology. There are promises of anonymity, independence from the existing banking system, and of course, significant return on investment. For many, cryptocurrencies are known as something that can make you rich if you had invested early in the development of a cryptocurrency. It is known that those who had bought Bitcoins by 2014 and didn't sell them until December 2017 made very significant profit. There were even cases where some people actually got rich. Something similar happened with other leading cryptocurrencies (and not only) such as Ethereum, Litecoin, Cardano, Solana, Axie Infinity, and the like.

At the same time, several people lost money. One of the reasons was because of their ignorance as they invested when the market prices of cryptocurrencies had reached the ceiling and then liquidated their investments at lower prices because they were afraid of losing everything. Another reason was that they fell victim to online fraud by hackers and others who deceived them in various ways. The blockchain and cryptocurrencies is a space with a lot of promises of high future returns, but it also has pitfalls, so a lot of people end up losing money.

Cryptocurrencies give an extremely high degree of freedom to move values at the push of a button, but, due to the lack of significant reforms, they have several loopholes that create monetary losses and more. It is an area that still has a long way to go to properly mature and find the right balance between that freedom and the right reforms that will protect people's investments in cryptocurrencies. Already over three hundred million people on the planet have invested in cryptocurrencies and by 2030, it is expected to exceed one billion. Hundreds of institutional investors have cryptocurrencies in their portfolios and give their clients analysis of their accounts in cryptocurrencies! The largest institutional investor, the multinational investment management firm Blackrock, which manages over ten trillion dollars in assets, now has cryptocurrencies in its portfolio.

Some of the world's largest companies have invested in cryptocurrencies directly or indirectly, according to blockdata.tech from September 2021 to June 2022:

Alphabet: $1.5 billion to Fireblocks, Dapper Labs, Voltage, Digital Currency Group

Blackrock: $1.17 billion to Circle, and Anchorage Digital

Morgan Stanley: $1.11 billion to Figment and NYDIG

Samsung: $979 million to Flowcarbon, Saga, Dank Bank, Yuga Labs, Big Whale Labs, Atomic Form, MYTY, FanCraze, Sky Mavis, Aleo, Ramper, Metrika, Animoca Brands

Goldman Sachs: $698 million to Certik, Coin Metrics, Elwood, Blockdaemon, Anchorage Digital

BNY MELLON: $690 million to Talos, Coin Metrics, Fireblocks

PayPal: $650 million to Talos, Layer Zero, TRM, Anchorage Digital

Microsoft: $477 million to Palm and ConsenSys

Commonwealth Bank: $421 million to Lygon, Xpansiv, Gemini

Tencent: $224 million to Oxalis, Ethernity, Showcon, Immutable

CITI: $215 million to Talos, TRM, Contour, Blockdaemon, Amberdata

Wells Fargo: $165 million to Talos and Elliptic

LG: $129 million to Jadu AR and The Sandbox

American Express: $115 million to TRM and Abra

The blockchain and cryptocurrencies is a space that is constantly booming due to its nature and the freedom it provides for creation, as well as the evolution of this technology. So, everyone can participate because the technology is evolving and blockchain services are constantly improving. This technology and the protocols that have been created have now laid the foundations for the creation of a fair, independent and free financial system that could either fully or partially replace the existing banking system or even work alongside it. Cryptocurrencies are also the biggest threat to the banking system and therefore face a major war, which may continue until banks adopt them. Several banks have already done so in many countries, such as the US, Australia, Brazil, Argentina, England, El Salvador, and others. Even the biggest critics, such as Warren Buffet, invest directly or indirectly. Warren Buffet is a major investor in the Brazilian online bank Nubank, which has over 60 million customers and gives them access to Bitcoin.

Cryptocurrencies are also known for their large price fluctuations. They can even go as low as -80% to -95% from their peak prices. This is to be expected even for Bitcoin and happens for various reasons such as market cycles, insecurity because it is something new, lack of concrete reforms from America, Europe, Australia, UK etc., market manipulation by speculators, and many other reasons. By reading this book, you will gain a greater understanding of all these, be able to predict them to a good extent, and handle them more correctly and at the right time.

Opportunities and risks

This space has huge opportunities, but to find them, one has to do proper research and evaluation, similar to what one would do for a listed company on the stock exchange. Pretty much the same rules apply in terms of the vision of the crypto project, the service or product it offers, the agents behind it, their whitepaper (something akin to a company's business plan), the competition, etc. Because this space is still new, there are opportunities like these that once existed. Today we would say in a phrase: "Like investing in Facebook, Google, Amazon and similar companies in 2000–2006." But there is a risk here, arising from people's emotional impulse (enthusiasm) to invest in a cryptocurrency because its price is going up a lot and then sell it because they see that its value is falling. So, in fear of losing everything, they end up liquidating their investment at a loss. They end up there because they don't understand what they are investing in and don't even know the basics of the cryptocurrency market or this particular project because of their lack of knowledge in finance, business, and investing. That's why I wrote this book, to help you understand more about this technology, the opportunities, the pitfalls, and how it works!

This book was created to provide a basic, yet comprehensive understanding of Blockchain and cryptocurrencies. In this book you will see the opportunities that exist in this industry, as well as the problems, pitfalls, risks, and every essential element that one needs to know in order to have a comprehensive understanding of this promising new technology. This information has been carefully compiled and collected after tens of thousands of hours of research over the last 10 years, through all my experience in this field.

Blockchain – Its Relation to Cryptocurrencies

What Is Blockchain?

In recent years, the term "Blockchain" has become increasingly popular. But what is blockchain? Simply put, a blockchain is mainly known as a digital ledger, meaning a collection of financial data for all transactions of each cryptocurrency. However, it is not only used in cryptocurrencies, as it has other important applications.

The name "Blockchain" was created from the words "block" and "chain," meaning a chain of blocks.

The blockchain is a database that is shared across a network of computers.

What Is a "Database"?

Most people have heard of databases, but many people don't know what they are. A database is a collection of data that computers can access. Data is organized in a systematic way so that it becomes easy to find and use.

There are many different types of databases. Some are used to store information about customers or products. Others are used to track financial transactions. Others are used to store medical records or research data.

Databases can be small and contain only a few hundred records. Or they may be very large and contain millions of records.

While the usual types of databases have the structure of Tables, where they store their data, Blockchain databases have the structure of Blocks (groups) of data linked together in Chains.

When a new piece of data is added to the blockchain database, it is encrypted, and a new block is added to the chain. Each block contains a link to the previous block, as well as a timestamp. This makes it impossible to modify data without changing all subsequent blocks, which requires consent from the network.

It grows continuously as completed blocks are added one after another when there is a new set of records. Each block contains a cryptographic hash of the previous block, a timestamp and the transaction data.

The hash pointer contains a value that points to the previous block, thus creating the chain. In addition, it also contains all the files of the previous block. So we can see how this element makes the blockchain extremely reliable and innovative.

This new system is a database that allows secure and transparent transactions. The potential applications of Blockchain are extensive and can bring revolution to many industries.

How Does Blockchain Work for Bitcoin?

It's actually quite simple. Bitcoin uses the blockchain to differentiate legitimate Bitcoin transactions from attempts to re-spend coins that have already been spent elsewhere. When someone buys or sells something using Bitcoin for example, the transaction is bundled together with others and becomes a mathematical puzzle. The solution to this puzzle – called a hash – is then added to the next block of data on the blockchain. This block is now permanent, searchable, and circulated to all computers on the Bitcoin network, so that everyone knows which Bitcoin belongs to whom.

So, we see that on the Bitcoin blockchain all transactions are visible and there is always transparency. One can see all the transactions that happen. Because of the nature of the blockchain, everything that happens will be seen. Thus, there can't really be any secret actions or movements of amounts. Even when people were robbed in the past, they were able to see where their Bitcoin went. This is how cybercrime agencies have been able to discover several cybercrimes.

It's really quite difficult for someone to commit a crime with the transparency that exists; not impossible, just difficult. If criminals want to move cryptocurrencies somewhere or buy something with them, it will be known immediately. And that's what makes the Bitcoin blockchain even more cool.

Decentralization

Decentralization is a key feature of Blockchain technology.

While traditional databases are centralized, meaning they are controlled by a single entity, blockchain databases are decentralized, meaning they are distributed across the network.

By definition, decentralization means that power in a system is distributed evenly among those who participate in it, rather than being concentrated in a single individual or group. In the blockchain context, decentralization refers to the fact that there is no central authority overseeing the network. Instead, the network is maintained by a decentralized network of computers, known as nodes, each of which has a copy of the blockchain.

Nodes are simply devices that are connected to the network and help it run smoothly. They can be computers, phones, servers, or anything else with an internet connection.

The nodes can be operated by anyone who wishes to join the network. Each node has a copy of the blockchain, and all nodes cooperate to verify and validate new transactions.

So, in short, decentralization refers to the distribution of power within a network, and nodes are devices that help keep the network running.

Decentralization has a number of advantages:

a) It makes transactions more valid because there is no point of failure. In order to be verified and confirmed, each transaction must be placed on a block that will follow very strict encryption rules, which are verified by the network. These rules prevent the modification of previous blocks, because this would invalidate all subsequent blocks. In this way, no person on the network can change what is included in the blockchain or replace parts of the blockchain to erase their own expenditures.

b) It allows censorship-resistant applications because there is no central authority that can censor or shut down the network.

c) The decentralized nature of Blockchain adds something extra to its security. There is no central point of control that hackers could exploit. Instead, the network is distributed across many different computers or nodes. This makes it much more resilient to attacks.

Blockchain Advantages

Since the launch of Bitcoin in 2009, Blockchain technology has been hailed as a revolutionary new way of managing data. Here are some of the key benefits of this innovative technology:

1. Increased security. This makes it an ideal solution for managing sensitive data.
2. Greater transparency.
3. More accuracy.

Use Cases of Blockchain

Blockchain is a distributed database that offers a secure, efficient, and decentralized way of storing data and conducting transactions. While the technology is still in its early stages and was first used in cryptocurrency applications, it has the potential to revolutionize a variety of industries such as healthcare, supply chain management, banking, and even voting.

Here are some of the most promising use cases for Blockchain technology.

Banking operations: Blockchain can help banks reduce costs and improve efficiency by better designing back-office operations and automating compliance processes.

Public services: Blockchain technology could be used to replace public services such as voting systems. This would create a more secure and transparent way of handling these important functions.

Saving money: if you want to save money while trading, Blockchain may be the answer. With Blockchain there is no need for an intermediary, which can help with reduced fees and savings.

Healthcare: Blockchain can help healthcare providers to securely store and share patient data while reducing fraudulent activity.

Supply chain management: Blockchain can help businesses track goods as they move through the supply chain from supplier to customer. This could help reduce lost goods and fraud, while improving transparency, responsibility, and accountability.

Origin of works of art or luxury goods: This can help someone ensure that these items are not fake and have not been stolen.

Transfer of property ownership: every transfer of property to another owner is recorded in the blockchain and there is transparency as to who owns the property at a given time. The entire history of transfers to date is also maintained, and can be searched, such as: previous owners, ownership percentages, type of ownership, and other details.

Digital contracts and agreements: For example, two parties could agree on terms and conditions and then codify those terms in a blockchain transaction. If either party tries to change the terms later, it will be seen because the transaction on the blockchain will no longer match.

Here are some examples of large companies that make use of Blockchain.

IBM is one of the largest technology companies in the world and is also one of the most active in Blockchain development. It has been working on

Blockchain projects for a while now and has a lot of experience to share. IBM is also a member of Hyperledger, which is a collaborative open-source effort (software code that can be freely modified and shared) to advance Blockchain technology.

Microsoft is another big company involved in Blockchain. It is working on many Blockchain-related projects, including Ethereum development tools and integration with the Azure cloud platform. Microsoft is also a member of Hyperledger.

Amazon is also involved in Blockchain with its Amazon Managed Blockchain service. It is partnering with other companies in Hyperledger to help develop this service.

Other big names already using Blockchain are Google, Walmart, Siemens, and Facebook. These companies are using Blockchain in various areas in their business, such as in their payments or in managing their products and inventory.

Blockchain Disadvantages

While Blockchain technology has many potential applications, there are also significant risks associated with its use.

One of the major disadvantages of Blockchain is its lack of scalability. The current design of the Blockchain limits it to processing about seven transactions per second. By comparison, Visa can process about 65,000 transactions per second. This scalability issue could limit the widespread adoption of Blockchain technology.

Another disadvantage of Blockchain is that it is often linked to illegal activities such as money laundering and drug trafficking. This is because Blockchain provides a level of anonymity that makes it difficult to monitor transactions. This could make it difficult for businesses to use Blockchain technology if they are required to comply with anti-money laundering regulations.

While the decentralized nature of Blockchain makes it very secure, it also makes it very difficult to change or undo transactions. This could be a problem if a mistake is made.

Blockchain technology requires a lot of computing power and energy to operate. This could make its use prohibitively expensive for some organizations.

In the world of Blockchain, regulations are a constant concern. The problem with Blockchain regulations is that they are a global phenomenon. Any attempt to set rules to regulate it will likely have to be coordinated between countries, which is not an easy task. Even if regulations are put in place, there is no guarantee that they will be effective. After all, Blockchain is designed to be decentralized and distributed, which makes it difficult to control. However, many believe that regulations are necessary to prevent abuse and ensure consumer protection. Without some kind of oversight, it is possible that some users will exploit the technology for malicious purposes.

Despite these drawbacks, Blockchain remains a promising technology with a lot of potential.

Conclusion

In conclusion, Blockchain is a powerful tool that can be used to create transparency and accountability in many industries. Its ability to track and verify transactions makes it an ideal solution for cryptocurrencies, supply chain management, food safety, and other areas where data integrity is critical.

While Blockchain is still in its early stages of development, the potential applications of this technology are endless. With the right regulations and governance in place, Blockchain could revolutionize the way we live and work. Its potential uses are likely to grow, holding great promise for the future.

The Bitcoin

The Beginning of Bitcoin

The dollar is controlled by the Federal Reserve and all other currencies are controlled in a similar way. Bitcoin is based on the Blockchain, which is not controlled by anyone, so you can't do whatever you want with it. If something happens to the banks or the financial system of the country, then all the customer information in the system can be transferred and used in any way the next bank or institution, that has authority over those accounts, likes. Also, if one lives in countries like Greece, with an unstable economy or banks that can collapse at any time, then the value of the country's currency becomes unstable and fear is created. As happened in 2009, when some of the Greek banks that had no cash reserves went bankrupt and then taxpayers' money was used to recapitalize them in order to bring some order to the financial system. In this way, a necessity was created for a monetary system that was not prone to such issues. Thus, Bitcoin was created to solve these problems, which, if left unsolved, would fall on the common man and he would pay the damage in the end.

Bitcoin, in addition to the above, can provide a fast financial system to all countries. It also provides access to services, companies, or even countries without any special tax and cost in money or time for simple transactions. These luxuries don't really exist out there, as anyone who has power because of their money can do whatever they want and charge as much as they want. Even governments fall prey to those who lend them money, but that's a topic for another book.

What Is Bitcoin?

Bitcoin is a digital currency created in January 2009 by an individual or group of individuals under the pseudonym Satoshi Nakamoto. No one officially knows who he or she is, but he or they created Bitcoin. A few years later, in 2013, the person or group disappeared after they had managed to get Bitcoin to a good level so that it could continue on its own as an idea. Bitcoin offers the idea of decentralized power, where there is no single individual or group deciding the future of the currency, and at least 51% of the network must decide on changes. At the same time, it offers the idea of lower fees or commissions and unbanked transactions. Most importantly, however, there is a constant amount of currency in circulation, which ensures that there will be no inflation.

Bitcoin has no physical existence, it is just some electronic money. All Bitcoin transactions are verified by a huge amount of computing power. Bitcoin coins are not issued or backed by banks or governments. Individual Bitcoins are not valuable as a commodity. However, many banks and governments are now very interested in this currency. Although it is not yet legalized money in most countries, Bitcoin is very popular and has caused the creation of hundreds of other cryptocurrencies, which we call altcoins, meaning different currencies from Bitcoin. Bitcoin is commonly abbreviated as "BTC" on various websites, blogs, and exchanges.

Basic Data About BTC

- There can only be 21,000,000 BTC coins.
- Bitcoin is the world's largest cryptocurrency by market capitalization. Anything that happens to BTC directly affects the entire market and every other cryptocurrency.

- Unlike fiat currency, Bitcoin is created, distributed, traded, and stored using a decentralized system of digital ledgers, which is the blockchain.
- Although it was created to function as a currency, it has gained more value and use as a work of art or some kind of asset than as a currency.
- At one point it reached a value of $68,789.63 per coin, but a few months later it dropped to around $20,000. Large fluctuations in price are one of its characteristics.
- It can't be controlled and changed by almost anyone, no matter how much power and money they have, and that's what makes it special.

Understanding Bitcoin

Simply put, since we've learned about the blockchain before, Bitcoin as a whole concept is simply a collection of computers (also referred to as "nodes" or "miners"), all running the Bitcoin code and storing its blockchain. A blockchain contains a collection, a chain of blocks. In each block there is a collection of transactions. Because all computers using the blockchain have the same list of blocks and transactions, they can transparently see these new blocks, which are filled with new Bitcoin transactions. Since everything has to agree with each other all the time, no one can cheat the system.

Anyone, whether running a Bitcoin node or not, can see these transactions taking place live. If someone wants to cheat or change something on the network, they would have to handle 51% of the computing power of the Bitcoin nodes. Bitcoin had over 100,000 nodes by 2021, and that number continues to grow, making such an attack quite unlikely and also cost prohibitive.

Even if someone manages to make such an attack, it will be meaningless since in a few minutes the miners will create a new line on the blockchain and everything that person has done will go offline. The power and authority will always be held by that 51% of the network.

Bitcoins as coins are held in public or private "keys" in the form of a code, which is a mathematical algorithm written in letters and numbers. The public key, which acts like a bank account number, serves as an address that is published to others so they can send Bitcoins. The private key is equivalent to a PIN for an ATM and is a code used only to authorize Bitcoin transfers. Bitcoin keys should not be confused with a Bitcoin wallet, which is a physical or digital device that facilitates Bitcoin transactions and allows users to track ownership of their coins. The term "wallet" is a bit misleading, as the decentralized nature of Bitcoin means that it is never stored "inside" a wallet, but decentralized on a blockchain.

Bitcoin uses peer-to-peer technology to facilitate direct payments. The independent individuals and companies who hold the dominant computing power and participate in the Bitcoin network as Bitcoin miners, and who are responsible for processing transactions on the blockchain, earn rewards from the release of new Bitcoin coins and transaction fees paid in Bitcoin. This is something that will be explained in more detail below.

These miners can be seen as a decentralized authority, which enhances the reliability of the Bitcoin network. New Bitcoin coins are released to the miners at a steady, but periodically decreasing rate. There are only 21 million Bitcoin coins and there will never be more, however not all 21 million are available now. The system works in a special way, where one has to make all these Bitcoins with their computer. The process to create them is called "mining." Of course, it is not possible for one computer to make them all, but everyone works together to mine Bitcoins. Since its creation until June 2022, about 19,067,868 Bitcoins have been mined, and all the rest remain to be mined.

This is the main difference with fiat currencies such as the Dollar, the Euro, etc. In central banking systems, the fiat currency is created at a rate that corresponds to the growth of goods, or at least that is the principle they say they have to operate on. This system is intended to maintain price stability. A decentralized system, such as Bitcoin's, sets the circulation rate in advance, according to an algorithm, and then this cannot be changed, which makes BTC increasingly rare. That's why it has such value as a currency.

Bitcoin Mining

Bitcoin mining is the process by which new Bitcoins are released into the market. Mining requires solving computationally difficult puzzles, which require enough computing power to discover a new block to be added to the blockchain. For each of these there is a reward in BTC.

Bitcoin mining adds and verifies transaction records across the network. The reward miners receive is halved after every 210,000 blocks. In 2009 block mining had a reward of 50 new Bitcoins. On May 11, 2020 it was halved for the third time, reducing the reward for mining each block to 6.25 Bitcoins. This makes this job more difficult and costly for miners, who must have large amounts of computing power to mine these Bitcoins.

There is a lot of work on the mining side. Companies like Intel have been producing products just for this job for the last few years. Entire factories have been built for Bitcoin mining, and the biggest cost, beyond buying the hardware, is the electricity to run all those computers.

One Bitcoin is divided into 100 million units (eight decimal places of Bitcoin) and this smallest unit is referred to as "Satoshi." This is done so that smaller amounts of BTC are available for transactions, as one can no longer use only large amounts of 5 or 10 BTC, because these are now of high value. It's like having only 50 or 100 dollar or euro notes in your wallet. That is why there must be smaller amounts of BTC to use for smaller value transactions. If necessary, and if the participating miners accept another change, Bitcoin could eventually be divided into even more decimal places.

Historical Facts of Bitcoin

August 18, 2008

The domain name of Bitcoin.org was registered. Of course, the identity of the person who registered it is not public information.

October 31, 2008

An individual or group using the name Satoshi Nakamoto makes an announcement to the cryptographic mailing list at *metzdowd.com*. This will become the beginning of how Bitcoin works today.

January 3, 2009

The first block of Bitcoin is mined, and it is block 0. It is also known as the "genesis block." It contains the following text: "The Times 03/Jan/2009 Chancellor on brink of second bailout for banks." ("The Times" is a UK newspaper)

January 8, 2009

The first version of the Bitcoin software is announced on the Cryptography mailing list.

January 9, 2009

Block 1 is mined and Bitcoin mining begins.

Who Is Satoshi Nakamoto?

Nobody knows who created Bitcoin. Satoshi Nakamoto is the name associated with the person or group of people who released the original Bitcoin white paper in 2008, which is the text that describes BTC. They worked on the original Bitcoin software released in 2009. In the years since, many people have either claimed to be or have been suggested as the real people behind the pseudonym, but until 2022 the real identity (or identities) behind Satoshi Nakamoto has not been found. We also know his, hers, or their BTC account, which is still active since he, she, or they decided to disappear.

Although we would like to believe that the genius who created Bitcoin was the first person to think of it, such innovations usually don't just happen. All major scientific breakthroughs, no matter how original, were based on pre-existing research. That's what happened with Bitcoin.

Before Bitcoin there was Adam Back's Hashcash, Nick Szabo's Bit Gold, and Hal Finney's Reusable Proof of Work. The Bitcoin white paper mentions Hashcash and b-money, as well as several other projects covering various areas of research. Of course, many of the people behind those projects could be on Satoshi's team, but no one knows for sure.

One reason that the inventor of Bitcoin kept his identity secret is privacy, to avoid too much attention from the media and national governments. Another reason is that, because of the attention from the media and governments, there is a high possibility that Bitcoin will cause significant disruption to current banking and monetary systems. This threat to the existing currency could prompt governments to take legal action against the creator of Bitcoin.

The other reason is safety. In 2009 alone, Satoshi and maybe a few other people mined 1,624,500 Bitcoins. The fact that they hold the majority of this asset could make them a target for criminals, especially because Bitcoins are less like stocks and more like cash, as the private keys needed to authorize payments can be kept anywhere in the house. The inventor of Bitcoin is likely to take proper precautions, be able to track any fraudulent transfers from his account, and eventually get his money back through the police after the criminals are found. However, remaining anonymous is a good way for Satoshi to limit his exposure to such attacks.

Now that we see how much power Bitcoin itself and all the other cryptocurrencies that follow Bitcoin have, it's generally a good thing that its creator is nowhere to be found. If he were known, it would affect the market in strange ways, and would certainly increase the negative attention on him, as such a person would have a lot of power. He would not only have the power of Bitcoin, but of all cryptocurrencies, as we are seeing. This is also a reason why Bitcoin has more value, in my opinion.

Investing in Bitcoin

Most Bitcoin supporters believe that this currency will be the future. Many individuals who support Bitcoin believe that it facilitates a much faster payment system with low transaction fees around the world. Although it is officially backed by only one government (El Salvador), as of this writing, Bitcoin can be exchanged with more familiar traditional currencies such as the US dollar. In fact, its exchange rate against the dollar attracts potential investors and traders (people who negotiate the buying and selling of a commodity, such as a currency) interested in making a lot of money quickly.

In March 2014, the IRS (Internal Revenue Service, the public financial agency of the US) stated that all cryptocurrencies, including Bitcoin, will be taxed as property and not as currency. As with any asset, the principle of buy low and sell high applies to Bitcoin. The most popular way to acquire Bitcoins is to buy from a Bitcoin exchange. There are also many other ways to earn and acquire Bitcoins.

Types of Risks Associated with Investing in Bitcoin

Although Bitcoin was designed to be a digital currency, it soon began to function as a regular stock investment. Some speculators were attracted to the digital currency because its value was very high, allowing them to make money easily. Thus, many people bought Bitcoin for its investment value rather than its original value, which was to act as a medium of exchange.

However, the risk is the lack of guaranteed value and the lack of a regulatory authority for Bitcoin and the cryptocurrency market in general. So, at any time, some group of people with a lot of money can "play" and do whatever they want with the prices, aiming of course for profit, without being restricted by any government or other authority.

The concept of virtual currency is still new. With their growing popularity, Bitcoin and other currencies are becoming less experimental and more realistic every day. Digital currencies are in a development phase. It is a high-risk investment, but also has a higher return than anything else out there right now.

There are many platforms that provide great benefits to anyone who lends them their Bitcoins for a period of time. Some give very large amounts, and are quite risky, so there is always the risk of losing all of one's Bitcoins on such platforms. Some others, like Binance for example, are safer platforms, as they have built a good level of operation and trust in the community.

Generally, an acceptable and good level of return from platforms where one can lend their Bitcoins is 5% to 7%. There are several platforms that will give such a rate, and they can give it either in Bitcoin or in some other currency, such as a stablecoin which has a fixed value, i.e., 1 to 1 with the US dollar.

This is a good opportunity for someone to profit from Bitcoin, not only by raising the general value of the currency, but also by lending their Bitcoins to get a steady return. Usually, these platforms can pay weekly or monthly, but in some cases, they pay the corresponding rate even per day.

The Risks of Investing in Crypto

To begin with, the idea of investing in Bitcoin or any other cryptocurrency is not a deterrent. However, Bitcoin and cryptocurrencies in general are competitors to the state currency and can be used for black market transactions, money laundering, illegal activities, or tax evasion. This could result in – and sometimes has resulted in – governments seeking to regulate, restrict, or even ban the use and sale of Bitcoin. This is why various rules are being put in place to address these issues, which may have implications for cryptocurrencies in general.

An example is when the New York State Department of Financial Services enacted certain regulations. These regulations require cryptocurrency companies to record the identity of their customers, have a compliance officer, maintain reserve funds, and transactions of $10,000 or more must be recorded and reported.

These regulations always cause turmoil in the market, which has a significant impact on the price of cryptocurrencies. Usually, all regulations have a long-term value, as they make cryptocurrencies safer and more stable. But at the stage we are in now, they cause turbulence in the markets, and also one cannot be sure what each state or country will do. They may suddenly decide to ban them, as China has done, and then the price will be affected greatly and for a long time.

In general, it is something that still needs time to get to a good point, although in 2022 both Europe and America seem to support cryptocurrencies and put in place regulations for security rather than restrictions.

Security Risk in Exchanges and Wallets

Most people who hold Bitcoin and other cryptocurrencies keep them on an exchange such as Binance or other cryptocurrency exchanges. These exchanges are completely digital and, as with any virtual system, are at risk from hackers, malware, and have operational problems.

A hacker can also gain access to someone's e-wallet and grab Bitcoin and other cryptocurrencies they hold. This is relatively simple, as long as they somehow obtain their electronic key or plant a virus on the victim's computer to gain access to their e-wallet. The safest thing to do is to keep them on a hard drive or USB stick that is not permanently connected to the internet.

But e-wallets are not necessarily dangerous. Only if someone gives away their electronic key or if they frequently enter websites with little protection or open links sent to them by strangers for no reason, can they be fooled. The computer holding someone's e-wallet is best operated with a fair amount of care. The user should only go to known pages, not open unknown links and not try too many new things. For example, he should not try a completely new exchange to which he will connect his wallet for the first time, as it may be made by a hacker with the intention of passing a virus or simply stealing his electronic key.

Exchanges have another issue that needs attention. Do the exchanges one uses have enough liquidity and some insurance coverage in case something goes wrong and a loss occurs?

Almost all exchanges have been attacked by hackers and have lost several Bitcoins and other cryptocurrencies. Even if this doesn't happen, when the market is down and liquidity is reduced on the exchange, someone may not be able to get their cryptocurrency back due to lack of liquidity on the exchange. The solution for this is, especially in the beginning, when we are just starting to learn about cryptocurrencies, to trust the big and secure exchanges, which have enough safety nets in case of a loss. Some of these exchanges are Binance, and KuCoin (at the time of writing, as this may change in the future). They are all three top exchanges in terms of turnover and quality in their work. They also have the strongest security programs to prevent any damage from hackers or due to lack of liquidity. Each of these exchanges has a special program to immediately manage large monetary losses that may occur, without putting their customers at risk, and without having to shut down their operations even for a moment.

These things are very important for an exchange, as we have seen many exchanges fail in the past because they have fallen victim to hackers or lack of liquidity, so everyone who had their money there lost it. But there may be safety in this area too. The three exchanges mentioned above are among the safest that I know of. They have very good customer service in case someone has a problem, which is very important for people new to the industry.

The reason why security is an important issue is because cryptocurrencies have something special about their transactions, that they are all permanent and irreversible. It's like cash: Any transaction made with Bitcoins can only be reversed if the person who received the Bitcoins decides to return them. There is no third party or payment processor, as there is with a debit or credit card – so there is no source of protection or recourse if there is a problem. This is what makes cryptocurrency transactions more special, and that's why we need to know the basics of cryptocurrency security.

Risks Around Investing in Bitcoin

In general, Bitcoin exchanges and Bitcoin accounts are not insured by any federal or government program. There are occasionally programs and companies working to create some security for cryptocurrencies, but so far there has not been anything that has any sort of government security.

While Bitcoin uses private key encryption to verify holders and record transactions, fraudsters may try to sell fake Bitcoins and use viruses to hack wallets and steal Bitcoins and other cryptocurrencies. There are many ways to steal from someone, but almost always the user must have given the scammers access first. In short, if someone is careful about which websites they visit and how they use the computer that holds their wallets, they run almost no risk. I say "almost no risk" because I will not underestimate the ingenuity and cleverness these people have to steal, but beyond a point of security there is nothing you can do, even if there was security from the state itself.

There have also been specific cases of Bitcoin price manipulation, which is another common form of fraud. In this case, some individuals agreed to crash the market and scare the holders of small amounts of Bitcoin and other cryptocurrencies. This resulted in the holders of small amounts of cryptocurrency selling them cheaper than they had bought them. The individuals who manipulated the market bought them cheaper and thereby made a profit. At this point, if governments were to put in place some rules like they do in the stock market, it would help a lot. In recent times, enough attention has been paid by many regulators to establish certain rules, but it is still not enough to prevent market manipulation and other tricks by fraudsters.

As with other investments, Bitcoin prices can fluctuate. Indeed, the value of the coin has seen wild fluctuations in price during its brief existence. In addition to high-volume buying and selling on exchanges, it has a high sensitivity to any new events. The price of Bitcoin can easily drop from 10% to 20% in a day. Of course, it can correspondingly go up as much.

If fewer people start accepting Bitcoin as a currency, these digital units may lose their value and become worthless. There has always been speculation that the "Bitcoin bubble" would burst. There were speculations when it was $3, when it was $250, when it was $17,000, and when it reached $65,000. Every time these speculations become intense when the market goes down and stop when the market goes up again. But over the years, generally speaking, its value just went up.

There is already enough competition. Although Bitcoin has a huge lead over the hundreds of other digital currencies that have emerged due to its brand recognition, there are several ways for someone to lose their money in such an investment in either Bitcoin or other cryptocurrencies. But that is the risk of entering an innovative market; a big risk but also a big reward if all goes well.

Scams Around the Bitcoin Issue

There are also many scams with the sole purpose of stealing from new investors who don't know much about cryptocurrencies.

A well-known way in which these scams work these days is with a call, usually from an unknown number from abroad. On the other end of the line is someone who promises to invest the person's money in various cryptocurrencies or stocks and make it skyrocket in value.

At this point we should know that these people are quite trained in the way they communicate and can really get someone to invest even if they are quite skeptical. They also have a plan, persistence, and good people-handling skills. The solution is clear: just hang up the phone. They have a plan for what to do if you yell at them, threaten them, and try to "screw them." Of course, if they understand that you're scared and can't put up much of a fight, that's definitely their best bet. It goes without saying that they have a bad purpose and you should not continue to talk to them even for fun, unless you want to lose large amounts of money in the end.

These people promise big profits, but they don't just stick to promises. After they get you to stay on the phone for a while and get to know each other, they will show you some platform to work on and everything will look right. They will also ask you for various documents to register on the platform, which will make the whole thing look more official and legitimate. It doesn't matter if it takes you days to do all this, they are playing for big bucks anyway and have the patience to do it.

You will then be asked to invest a sum of money. Here they expect you to put in a small amount, which can be from 200 dollars to a few thousand. Then you will see the amounts on the platform where they have set up your account and everything will look okay. Later, they will invest with your money or at least that is what the platform will show you. They will do it in such a way that it will look like you had big profits and some losses now and then.

Your 400 dollars can make you 625 one day, 587 the next, 750 the next and so on. It is important that the person will see that with a small amount of money they can actually make so much money. And of course, they will let him pull out a sum if he wants to, to really believe that all this is true. But that's where the real game starts for them.

Of course, I have to say that these platforms are made by them and, of course, they show you what they want to show you. So there's no real profit or investment, they just make it look that way. Then, after you believe that it's all actually real and that you really did earn money so easily, they convince you to do whatever it takes to find those large sums of money they were aiming for in the first place.

At this point they know that the person will do anything to get some big money! If someone went from 400 dollars to 625 dollars overnight, imagine what would happen if they had 400,000 dollars in it... This is also the point where you simply won't hear from them again. Someone, out of greed for an easy and quick profit or because of some necessity that has been created in one way or another, at this point will find a way to give large sums of money for this investment. After that, he is simply screwed for good.

This is the simplest form of deception practiced these days and these are the familiar phone calls that many of us have received from time to time. Sometimes the strategy changes a little bit, but in general it is what I have described.

One might think that this would never catch him as a fool and that even if he did get into something like this, he would not lose much. Here, I should say that in an interview I had with a lawyer on my YouTube show on the subject, he revealed to me that the average amount of money his clients have lost from this strategy was about 100,000 dollars. Not a small amount for a country like Greece.

This shows that once they manage to fool someone, it is very simple to convince them to do anything to get huge sums of money. It also shows that they have a very good strategy. So the only solution with them is really to hang up on them, as they can use every trick in the book to get us to stay on the phone, where they will eventually get us.

They also usually don't stop there. Later, they may call again, in the form of the police, the bank, or some authority in general, and they will get the person to give them money again in the hope that they will get back what they have lost. Of course, they don't really care if they succeed in any of the above steps, because for them it's just math. They know for sure that out of every 100 calls they make, 5 for example will pay and one of them will make a lot, so it's worth their while.

This is just one example of the many scams that exist. Another well-known practice in this regard is when they steal our data and passwords through a link that can be reached via email, phone, or a social media message. In this practice, they simply steal all the data, but only if the user gives them permission by clicking on the link.

In this case, we will receive a link, for example on our mobile phone, which, for various reasons, will ask us to click on it. After that, it asks us to enter some data or confirm something and then they manage to access our codes with our permission.

Very simple practice and its solution is even simpler: just don't click on every link that arrives with any message on your mobile phone. We're pretty careful with these. If it's from a person we know, it's good to make sure that it's really that person and that they haven't fallen victim to a scammer who sent us that link using our friend's profile.

The age of speed also requires a lot of attention, good control, and knowledge of all this. We want fast transactions, but we also need to know how to make fast decisions. How can we check something quickly to see if it is reliable or another scam? Of course, since we're talking about investments, the biggest scam is advertising that someone in one transaction, overnight or in a week, became a millionaire or made a lot of money!

There is simply no such thing. Whoever has succeeded, let's just consider him as one of the lucky ones who won the first lottery ticket respectively and nothing more.

Bitcoin has made the biggest leap as an asset. If someone had invested $1000 in 2010, today they would have about $300 million (at the time of writing). But what does this mean? It means nothing.

That $1,000, the next day it might be worth $50 and for several weeks it might be worth less than the $1,000 he had put in at the beginning. Practically, it would have taken more than 12 years of patience to have that $300 million. There is hardly anyone who would have the patience to hold them and not sell them when they became $500 or $5,000 or $50,000. So the advertisement that someone made it and kept it and became rich can only teach us that patience helps sometimes, but in no way can someone make that much money in a few hours, days, or weeks without doing anything, except of course for some lucky people who would have the same chances of winning if they played other lucky games.

Investing in cryptocurrencies is high risk, which means you can lose a lot of money in many ways. But it also happens the opposite, to win a lot of money in many ways. It takes study, patience, and a lot of logic.

Another good feature in this area is not to consider that one has missed the opportunity of a lifetime by not getting into an investment early or getting out early. He should not be upset about this, he should not let it affect him at all. When he succeeds in this, he will make many good investments and fewer bad ones.

And maybe one day, after many investments, some of which he will lose and some of which he will win, who knows, he will be lucky enough to really multiply the value of his money by 1,000, 10,000, or 100,000. But I think that can happen later, after a lot of investing and after he has gained enough friction in the subject. But until then, let's keep an eye on the basics and not go straight for the big stuff, since we don't know the rules of the game very well yet.

What Happens When There Are Disagreements in the Cryptocurrency Community

Since the release of Bitcoin, there have been many instances of disagreements between factions of miners and developers, which have caused major disruptions in the cryptocurrency community. In some of these cases, Bitcoin user and miner groups have changed the protocol of the Bitcoin network itself.

This process is known as "forking" and usually results in the creation of a new type of Bitcoin with a new name. Forking can be a "hard fork," where a new currency shares its transaction history with Bitcoin up to a decisive point of separation, at which point a new token is created at that point. Examples of cryptocurrencies that have been created as a result of a hard fork include Bitcoin cash (created in August 2017), Bitcoin gold (created in October 2017), and Bitcoin SV (created in November 2017).

A "soft fork" is a change to the protocol, which is still compatible with previous system rules. It only adds whatever new thing is needed to the new currency or token. This does not affect the original Bitcoin; it just creates a new token on top of it, which continues on its own network. It can't change anything in the existing Bitcoin; it just uses part of its blockchain, so to speak, and continues with the rules that the core group of developers or miners who made it want.

Other cryptocurrencies that are decentralized work in a similar way. It's not a big deal, as it may not change the value of the original currency much, but it's a fact that happens and is a solution to any disputes over decentralized networks.

Proof of Work (PoW) and Proof of Stake (PoS)

What Is Proof of Work (PoW)?

Proof of Work (PoW) is the way Bitcoin and other similar cryptocurrencies work. It describes a system that requires an effort that is feasible, but cannot be considered trivial, in terms of preventing frivolous or malicious uses of computing power, such as sending spam or other types of attacks. The concept was subsequently adapted to secure digital money in 2004 using a hash algorithm.

Proof of Work was originally created as a proposed solution to the growing problem of spam emails. After its introduction in 2009, Bitcoin became the first widely implemented application of the PoW idea. Proof of Work is now the basis of many other cryptocurrencies, enabling secure, decentralized consensus.

Basic data for the Proof of Work

- Proof of Work is a decentralized consensus mechanism that requires the members of a network to make efforts to solve an arbitrary mathematical puzzle in order to prevent someone from "playing" the system.
- Because of Proof of Work, transactions in Bitcoin and other cryptocurrencies can be processed peer-to-peer in a secure manner, without the need for approval from a trusted third party.

- Proof of Work is widely used in cryptocurrency mining, for transaction validation and mining new tokens.
- Proof of Work requires huge amounts of energy, which increases when more miners join the network.
- There is also Proof of Stake (PoS), which is one of the many new consensus mechanisms that have been created as an alternative to the problems of Proof of Work.

As we said before, Bitcoin is a digital currency backed by a type of distributed ledger known as a blockchain. This ledger contains a record of all Bitcoin transactions, arranged in sequential "blocks" so that no user is allowed to make malicious changes. If there is a modified version, then it is quickly rejected by other users.

The way users detect the breach is through hashing. Hashing is a one-way operation: it cannot be used to obtain the original data, but only to check whether the data that created the hash matches the original data.

Creating any hash for a set of Bitcoin transactions would be trivial for a modern computer. So, in order to turn the process into a "job," the Bitcoin network sets a certain level of difficulty. This setting is adjusted so that a new mined block is added to the blockchain creating a valid hash.

Mining is a competitive process, but we would say it is more of a lottery than a race. The project itself is arbitrary. For Bitcoin, it involves iterations of specific hashing algorithms, which are of the SHA-256 type (a cryptographic hash function that produces a nearly unique 256-bit hash). Only the winner of a round of hashing, however, aggregates and records transactions from the transaction cache (mempool) to the next block. Because the winner is chosen randomly, depending on the work done, this system incentivizes everyone in the network to act honestly and record only true transactions.

Miners are gathering to increase their chances of mining blocks, which creates transaction fees and, for a limited time, a reward for new Bitcoins created.

Proof of Work makes it extremely difficult to change any aspect of the blockchain, as such a change would require the re-mining of all subsequent blocks. It also makes it difficult for a user or group of users to monopolize the computing power of the network, because the machinery and power required to complete the hashing operations is extremely expensive.

In short, Proof of Work requires nodes in a network to provide evidence that they have spent computing power (i.e., work) in order to reach consensus in a decentralized manner and thus prevent the network from being bypassed by bad actors.

Why do cryptocurrencies need Proof of Work?

Cryptocurrency blockchains, because they are decentralized and peer-to-peer by design, require some way to achieve consensus and security. Proof of Work is such a method that makes the use of resources too intensive for someone trying to bypass the network. There are also other proof mechanisms that require fewer resources but have other drawbacks or flaws, such as Proof of Stake (PoS) and Proof of Burn (PoB). Without a proof mechanism, the network and the data stored on it would be vulnerable to attack or theft.

What Is Proof of Stake (PoS)?

The concept of Proof of Stake (PoS) states that a person (computer) can mine or validate transactions in blocks according to how many coins they hold and not according to their computing power. This means that the more coins the miner owns, the more mining power he has.

In a nutshell:

- Proof of Stake was created as an alternative to Proof of Work, which is the original consensus algorithm in blockchain technology, and is used to confirm transactions and add new blocks to the chain.

- Proof of Work requires huge amounts of energy, with miners selling their coins to eventually pay the bill. Proof of Stake gives mining power based on the percentage of coins the miner owns.
- With Proof of Stake, cryptocurrency miners can mine or validate transaction blocks based on the number of coins they hold.
- Proof of Stake is considered less risky in terms of the miner's ability to attack the network, because it structures the compensation in such a way as to make an attack less advantageous for the miner.
- While most cryptocurrencies now work with Proof of Stake, Bitcoin, the largest cryptocurrency, is based on Proof of Work rather than Proof of Stake.

What Is the Difference Between Proof of Work and Proof of Stake?

Proof of Stake was created as an alternative to the concept of Proof of Work to solve various problems, such as the large amount of energy consumed by the Proof of Work network. When a transaction is initiated, the transaction data is placed in a block with a maximum capacity of 1 megabyte and then copied to multiple computers or nodes in the network. The nodes are the administrative body of the blockchain and verify the legitimacy of the transactions in each block.

Mining requires a lot of computing power to perform different cryptographic calculations to unlock the computational challenges. The computing power translates into a large amount of electricity and power required for Proof of Work.

It has been estimated that the Bitcoin network spends large amounts of electricity for each transaction or mining of new currency. One transaction has come to require more than the amount of electricity needed to power a typical American household for a day. This number is constantly increasing, so more efficient solutions have been called for. That's why the new cryptocurrencies don't work with Proof of Work.

Proof of Stake seeks to address this issue by attributing the mining power to the percentage of coins held by the miner. In this way, instead of using energy to solve the puzzle as in the Proof of Work, a Proof of Stake miner is limited to mining a transaction rate that reflects the ownership stake of the cryptocurrency he or she owns.

The problem with Bitcoin, which uses a Proof of Work system, is that at some point in the future there may be fewer miners available due to little or no reward from Bitcoin mining. The only fees they can earn will come from transaction fees, but these will decrease over time as users choose to pay lower fees for their transactions.

With fewer miners than needed to mine coins, the network becomes more vulnerable to a 51% attack, as mentioned in a previous chapter.

With a Proof of Stake, an attacker would need to acquire 51% of the cryptocurrency to perform a 51% attack, meaning that they would need to have 51% of all Bitcoins if they are to work with this system. Proof of Stake avoids this "tragedy" because it makes it unprofitable for a miner with a 51% stake in cryptocurrency to attack the network. Although it would be difficult and costly to accumulate 51% of a trusted digital currency, a miner with a 51% stake in that currency would have no interest in attacking a network in which he owns most of it. If the value of the cryptocurrency falls, it means the value of its holdings will fall. Thus, the holder of the majority of the coins will have more incentive to maintain a secure network.

Could Bitcoin be changed to Proof of Stake?

There is a debate that it is almost impossible for Bitcoin to switch to Proof of Stake due to some technical challenges involved in the transition from one system to another. This change would really hurt those who have put the most effort into Bitcoin at the moment. However, in theory, many predict that eventually, Bitcoin will move to a Proof of Stake model.

Investment Strategies

The best thing about investment strategies is that they are flexible. If you choose one that doesn't fit your risk tolerance or your schedule, you can certainly make changes. But of course, that usually comes at a high cost. Every purchase carries a fee. Also, selling assets can generate capital gains and those gains are taxable and therefore expensive.

At the same time, someone who has never invested before should bear in mind that they will lose money in the beginning, no matter how well trained they are. I am not saying this to discourage anyone from investing to make money. However, since the initial idea one has when considering investing is that it will make money, one should keep in mind that in order to make good money from something like this, one will often happen to lose money, no matter how much education or study one has done on the subject.

The real cost of learning how to invest is the money one loses at the beginning, the heartache, headache, fear and nerves of lost opportunities, wrong investments, and wrong buying and selling points. These are the real costs in the beginning. But if one overcomes them and endures, then the study one has done, the education one has paid for, and also the investment of one's time and money begins to make sense. He just needs to go through that experience in the beginning. Of course, there are exceptions to the rule, where for some people everything works out, but I'm talking to you about the beaten path, since I went through it myself.

So, beyond that, let's look at four common investment strategies that suit most investors. By taking the time to understand the characteristics of each strategy, you'll be in a better position to choose the one that's right for you in the long run, without having to incur the cost of changing course.

Before you start researching your investment strategy, it is important to gather some basic information about your financial situation. Ask yourself these basic questions and write down the answers on a piece of paper:

- What is your current financial situation, how much do you earn and what funds do you have?
- What is your cost of living, including monthly expenses and debts?
- How much can you afford to invest, both initially and on an ongoing basis?

Although you don't need a lot of money to get started, you should look at your financial capacity to do so. If you have a lot of debt or other obligations, it may be important to find an additional source of income so that you can put money aside.

Make sure you can afford to invest before you start putting money in, especially because when there is no financial comfort and the market falls, then there is a lot of fear and this leads people to make mistakes. One has to be able to keep their cool in this game. If he is being chased by debts or has no money for the basics in his house, then it doesn't seem like he could do that.

Then set your goals. Everyone has different needs, so you need to determine what yours are. Do you plan to save for retirement? Are you interested in making large purchases in the future, such as a house or a car? Do you want financial freedom? Do you dream of becoming a millionaire? This will help you create a strategy.

Find out what your risk tolerance is. This is usually determined by several key factors, such as your age, your income, and how long you have until retirement. The younger someone is, the more risk they can take. More risk means higher returns, while lower risk means the gains won't be realized as quickly. But keep in mind, high-risk investments also mean there's a greater chance of losses.

Finally, learn the basics. It is essential to have a good understanding of the subject you are dealing with, so that you do not invest blindly.

Strategy 1: Value Investing

Value investors are chasing opportunities. They seek out cryptocurrencies that they believe are undervalued. They seek out cryptocurrencies that they believe their price does not fully reflect their value. Value investing is based, in part, on the idea that there is some degree of irrationality in the market. This irrationality, in theory, presents opportunities to acquire an asset at a discounted price and make money from it when it rises to its normal price or even higher.

It is not necessary for value investors to explore large volumes of financial data to discover a hidden gem. Because of the large amount of data in new cryptocurrency projects, one can simply look at the basics, such as the team and the goals of the project, so that one can have an idea of whether or not it is worthwhile.

Investors can change strategy at any time, but doing so, especially as a value investor, can be costly. However, many investors abandon the strategy after a few months of poor performance, or in the case of equities, after a few years of poor performance. The lesson here is this: to succeed in value investing you have to play the big game; you have to look into the future and be able to see if the project you chose could survive and grow as you would like.

But, if you are a true value investor, you don't need anyone to convince you that you should stay in it for the long term, because this strategy is designed around the idea that you should buy businesses and not stocks or cryptocurrencies. That means the investor needs to look at the big picture, not a temporary return. People often cite legendary investor Warren Buffet as the epitome of a value investor. He has been doing his studies sometimes for years. But when he's ready, he goes with the largest amount he can afford and commits for a long time.

In this strategy you need to think long term. The picks are based on decade-long trends, with decades of future performance in mind. You need to see which companies, in your opinion, will be there in the future and which will make a difference by rising to the top in terms of value.

Strategy 2: Growth Investing

Rather than seeking low-cost deals, growth investors want investments that offer strong upside potential in terms of future equity earnings. It could be said that a growth investor is often looking for the "next big thing." Growth investors, however, do not mindlessly embrace speculative investments. Instead, they involve assessing the current health of a stock, as well as its potential to grow.

A growth investor looks at the prospects of the industry in which the stock thrives. You might ask, for example, if there is a future for electric vehicles before investing in Tesla. You might wonder if A.I. (Artificial Intelligence) will become part of our daily lives before investing in a technology company. There must be evidence of a broad and strong public desire for the company's services or products to show that it is going to grow. Investors need to answer this question to see if it has a future. Simply put: A growth stock should have increasing value. The company should have a consistent trend of strong earnings and revenues that indicate the ability to meet growth expectations.

But that's true for stocks, so how does it work with cryptocurrencies? In cryptocurrencies one has to look at the product that each cryptocurrency project gives. Some offer physical, real products that one can see and touch, while others offer intangible services such as digital artwork or Web 3.0.

Another thing to check is how much of an audience a project has on social media and whether that audience is growing over time. This way one sees if there is interest in that project. The next thing that plays a role is the team behind the project. If they have any experience in successful projects in the past, that will help.

This is because so far, most cryptocurrency projects are new and do not even have a physical product, which makes it more difficult to evaluate. We could say that in a way the entire cryptocurrency market falls into this category, since most projects are new and operate with the aim of having some value in the future.

Is Growth Investing working?

Value investments tend to outperform growth investments in the long run. This does not mean that a growth investor cannot benefit from the growth strategy. It simply means that a growth investment does not typically produce the level of returns seen with a value investment.

Some critics of growth investments warn that "growth at any price" is a dangerous approach. Such a move caused the tech bubble, which turned millions of portfolios into thin air.

It is important to keep in mind that at the first sign of a downturn in the economy, growth stocks are often the first to be hit.

Development investors should also carefully consider the management capacity of the executive team of such a project. Achieving growth is one of the most difficult challenges for a business. Therefore, it is required to have a leadership team in place. It is also very easy to create a false image of growth with social media, which makes it a little more difficult to properly assess the growth that such a project has or will have. Investors need to monitor how the team is performing and the means by which it is achieving growth. Growth has little value if it is achieved with heavy borrowing and large expenditures on advertising alone without a meaningful product.

So here the investment product becomes an issue again. I make it an issue because it's the most difficult part of any cryptocurrency project.

At the same time, investors will need to assess the competition. A company may enjoy stellar growth, but if its main product is easily replicated, the long-term prospects are dim.

The GoPro camera is a prime example of this phenomenon. Its once excellent stock has subsequently seen regular annual revenue declines. Much of this collapse is attributed to the easily replicable design. After all, GoPro is, at its core, a small camera in a box. In addition, the company has failed to design and release new products, a necessary step to sustain growth – something growth investors should consider.

In cryptocurrencies, we see this many times with various projects that promise education or a decentralized economy. Now all the projects in cryptocurrencies do this. There is a lot of education and a lot of decentralized economy projects. The question is, what else will all these projects create to show that they are working for the future?

Strategy 3: Momentum Investing – Hype

Think of momentum investors as technical analysts. This means they use a strictly data-driven approach to trading and look for patterns in cryptocurrency prices to guide their buying decisions. In essence, momentum investors act in defiance of the "Efficient Market Hypothesis" (economic theory where investors base their decisions on the assumption that financial markets are information efficient).

Traders following such a strategy must be fully prepared to buy and sell at any time. Profits are generated in weeks and months, not years.

There is a specific way they work, and it is as follows.

Shorting

Aggressive momentum traders can use short selling as a way to boost their returns. The practice of short selling in finance is the sale of assets, usually securities, that the short seller has "borrowed" from a third party with the intention of buying identical securities later to return them to the lender.

This technique allows an investor to profit from a fall in the price of an asset. I will give this example with stocks to make it easier to understand, but in cryptocurrencies it is done in exactly the same way and more easily. For example, the short seller, believing that the price of a security will fall, borrows 100 shares totaling $1000. The short seller then immediately sells these shares on the market for $1000. He then waits for the price of the asset to fall. When this happens, he buys back the 100 shares (so that they can be returned to the lender) for, say, $250. Therefore, the short seller made $1000 on the initial sale, then spent $250 to buy the shares back for a profit of $750.

The problem with this strategy is that there is unlimited risk. In a normal investment, the downside risk is the total value of your investment. If you invest 1000 dollars, the maximum you can lose is 1000 dollars. However, with short selling, the maximum possible loss is unlimited. In the above scenario, for example, you borrow 100 shares and sell them for $1000. But the stock may not fall as expected. Instead, it goes up. Now the 100 shares may be worth $1500, then $2000 and so on. Sooner or later the short seller has to buy the shares again to return them to the lender.

Of course, this is one way that one can make profits faster, but also lose them faster. It takes a lot of education and the truth is that there is a lot of misinformation about this strategy, because it is also the strategy most used for scams and quick money. There is a lot of hype.

Strategy 4: Dollar Cost Averaging (DCA)

Dollar Cost Averaging (DCA) is the practice of making regular investments in the market over time and is not mutually exclusive to the other methods described above. Rather, it is a means of executing whatever strategy one chooses. It is also the strategy that helps someone who doesn't have a lot of money to get into large investments all at once. With DCA, you can choose to put 50 dollars or 100 dollars or 500 dollars into an investment account every month. Generally, one invests as much money as one has available so that, over time, a large amount of investment is accumulated. This disciplined approach becomes especially powerful when you use automated features that invest on your behalf. It's easy to commit to a plan when the process requires almost no oversight.

The advantage of the DCA strategy is that it avoids the laborious and unfortunate strategy of market timing. With this strategy, you don't care what phase of the market you are in and whether you make a small or big mistake. Even experienced investors are occasionally tempted to buy when they think prices are low, only to discover, to their dismay, that they may fall further.

When investments are made with regular increases, the investor achieves prices at all levels, from high to low. These periodic investments essentially reduce average purchase costs and risk.

A Wise Choice

The DCA is a wise choice for most investors. It keeps you committed to saving while reducing the level of risk and the impact of volatility. But for those who are able to invest a good lump sum, DCA may not be the best approach. It's usually a good option for people who don't have large amounts of money set aside.

Most investors are not in a position to make a single, large investment. Therefore, DCA is suitable for most people. In addition, a DCA approach is an effective way to remain unaffected by market ups and downs. You don't particularly care if you bought at a downturn or at the highest point, since the investment is usually a small amount of money and you are buying all the time, so you will be in all market ranges. It greatly reduces the risk and stress that a new investor may have. This has a lot of value in the long run, because the person himself does not accumulate a lot of defeats in the matter. He has both gains and losses. This makes him have a better understanding of the subject, so later he can play his moves more correctly.

The DCA circumvents these common problems by removing human weaknesses from the equation. It provides good insight into the market cycle and creates a really good investment character. After 2 years of DCA, where one consistently puts in 200 dollars every month, one now knows what is happening in the market to a large extent and is ready for larger investments without fear.

Once You Have Defined Your Strategy

In this way you can identify a strategy or a combination of strategies that will be right for you. However, there are still a few things you need to do before making your first deposit on the project you are interested in.

First, work out how much money you need to cover your investments. This includes how much money you can deposit in the beginning, as well as how much you can continue to invest in the future. Ideally, it should be money that won't hurt you if you lose it. This is for many reasons. One reason is that if someone loses everything in a few days because they didn't calculate something correctly (a very common mistake), it's much harder to look at the mistake objectively, correct it, and make some investment again later. He'll mostly think about the defeat he suffered by one fall the first time.

Then you need to decide the best way to invest.

Think about what your investment vehicles are. Remember that it doesn't help to keep all your eggs in one basket, so make sure to spread your money across different investment vehicles by diversifying your cryptocurrencies. Here, I will add that cryptocurrencies are just a branch. So, you can also split your investment into different branches, like stocks, bonds, real estate, and anything else. If the other categories seem difficult for you to invest in because they require quite large amounts of money, I should point out that one can now buy pieces of real estate for less than $100 and receive monthly returns on their capital. Now is the time to figure out what you want your investment portfolio to consist of and what you want it to look like.

The investment is a roller coaster, so keep your emotions away. It can seem amazing when your investments make money, but when they have a loss, it can be hard to manage. That's why it's important to take a step back, take your emotions out of the equation, and read as much as you can on the subject on a regular basis to make sure you're on track.

Education in this area, combined with experience, is what will make you a winner!

The Bottom Line

The decision to choose a strategy is more important than the strategy itself. Indeed, any of these strategies can generate significant returns, provided the investor makes a choice and commits to it. The reason it is important to choose is that the sooner you get started, the greater the results of your strategy will be, and discipline in a strategy will get you out of a crisis or any bad situation.

Remember, don't focus solely on annual returns when choosing a strategy. Follow the approach that fits your schedule and your risk tolerance. Overlooking these aspects can lead to a high abandonment rate and often result in a change of strategies when you should simply stick to your original strategy. Numerous changes create costs that reduce the annual rate of return. Formulate your strategy and show perseverance and discipline. Of course, you also need to create a long-term plan because, as I mentioned earlier in the book, there are no people who became rich from these investments overnight. If there are, they are only the exception and would have had the same chances of winning those millions in the lottery.

What Is Trading?

Trading is a basic economic concept that involves the buying and selling of goods and services, with compensation paid by a buyer to a seller or by exchanging cryptocurrencies, goods, or services between the parties. Trading can take place in an economy between producers and consumers. International trading allows countries to expand markets for both goods and services that would otherwise not be available. This is why an American consumer can choose between a Japanese, German, or American car. As a result of international trading, the market includes more competition and therefore more competitive prices, which brings a cheaper product to the consumer.

In financial markets, trading refers to the buying and selling of securities, such as buying and selling shares on the New York Stock Exchange (NYSE). In the cryptocurrency markets, trading refers to the buying and selling of cryptocurrencies, such as buying and selling cryptocurrencies on the Binance exchange.

What Is Cryptocurrency Trading?

Cryptocurrency trading is, in short, the ability to predict in various ways how the value of a cryptocurrency will move in the next hour, day, week, or even month and make a profit from it. If you perceive it will go high, buy now when it's low and sell later when it's high. If you think it will go lower soon, sell now and buy more of the same cryptocurrency for less money when it goes down in value.

Cryptocurrency trading involves speculation related to the price fluctuations of cryptocurrencies. It can be done in two ways. One is simply by buying and selling the coins present on an exchange. The other is through a CFD (Contract For Difference) account, which is a financial contract that pays the differences in settlement price between the opening and closing transactions of the currency.

Trading has its own theory. As a subject, it contains a lot of data and practices that one needs to study and learn how to understand the data, as one will need to deal with the technology involved.

CFD Transactions in Cryptocurrencies

CFDs allow investors to trade on the price movement of securities and derivatives. Derivatives are financial investments that are derived from an underlying asset. Essentially, CFDs are used by investors to bet on whether the price of the underlying asset or security will increase or decrease.

CFD traders can bet on the price to rise or fall. Traders who expect the price to rise will buy the CFD, while those who see the price moving down will sell an open position.

CFD trades are derivatives, which allow you to speculate on the price movements of cryptocurrencies without taking ownership of the underlying currencies. You can go long (buy) if you think a cryptocurrency will rise in value or short (sell) if you think it will fall.

Buying and Selling Cryptocurrencies Through an Exchange

When you buy cryptocurrencies through an exchange, you are buying the cryptocurrencies themselves. You will need to create an account on the exchange, put the full value of the asset to open a position, and store the cryptocurrency tokens in your own wallet until you are ready to sell. Many exchanges have limits on how much money you can deposit.

There are also applications that are linked to the exchanges and help with trading. One makes the desired trading strategy on the chosen exchange and then the app simply makes the purchases or sales on behalf of the user.

There is a lot of data and information on this issue. One has to study enough to be able to build their own strategy or find one that really works most of the time.

This is a fun way to make some money, but it doesn't have much to do with actual investing. It's just a trick to make some money by correctly predicting where the market will go.

New to Cryptocurrencies

In this chapter we will learn the basics for someone who is new to cryptocurrencies, to sort out the information and data they need to get started in the right order and as safely as possible in this new world.

The aim is to bring order to all the chaos and the volume of information that exists on the internet and everywhere around us.

The first thing you need to familiarize yourself with is the *CoinMarketCap.com* website. There is also a mobile app.

CoinMarketCap

CoinMarketCap is a price-tracking website with the world's most references for cryptoassets in the fast-growing cryptocurrency space. Its mission is to make cryptoassets traceable and efficient globally. It empowers retail users with unbiased, high-quality, and accurate information to draw their own informed conclusions.

It was founded by Brandon Chez in May 2013. CoinMarketCap quickly grew to become the most trusted source by users, organizations, and media for comparing thousands of cryptoassets. It is commonly cited by CNBC, Bloomberg, and other major news outlets. Even the US government uses CoinMarketCap data for research and reporting!

In April 2020, CoinMarketCap was acquired by Binance Capital Mgmt.

The website Coinmarketcap.com really has everything about cryptocurrencies.

But what does "everything" mean?

It has training in almost every area of cryptocurrency and is free. It has an option where you can read articles from the biggest and most authoritative blogs about cryptocurrencies. It displays information about almost all cryptocurrencies available in the market. It adds many new cryptocurrencies daily. This does not mean that it is a website from which you buy cryptocurrencies, although it gives the options and all the information one needs to buy any cryptocurrency. It is a website that, to put it very simply, contains a search option and websites for every cryptocurrency that exists. Of course, there are other websites like *Coinmarketcap.com*, but for me, this is the easiest and most useful.

What is important to know about Coinmarketcap is that it works like a search engine, like Google, but for the cryptocurrency world. For example, you type the word Bitcoin into the search and it shows you everything about Bitcoin.

Some information you can see there is:

- The price of a cryptocurrency
- A graph with its price from 2013
- A chat, where anyone can write their ideas about it
- All the information available about the project
- Where it is available for purchase and at what prices
- What stock each cryptocurrency exchange has
- The latest articles from the major cryptocurrency websites and blogs
- Similar projects
- Options that will help you buy safely, step by step

- And many other data

It really has everything. So, the first thing you need to familiarize yourself with is the Coinmarketcap website, which, for me, is the most useful tool for the cryptocurrency world. The best part is that it is equally useful for both a beginner and a professional in cryptocurrency.

After you have gained some familiarity with buying cryptocurrencies through the Coinmarketcap website, you should also have a wallet for your cryptocurrencies. The one I recommend for starters is Binance. There are so many exchanges and wallets, but there is a difference between them. An exchange is a website or app where you can exchange or buy cryptocurrencies for fiat money (fiat in simple terms is "regular" money like the dollar and the euro), but also store your cryptocurrencies. Wallets are applications where one can simply hold their cryptocurrencies. You can send or receive cryptocurrencies from a wallet and connect it to other platforms and websites, but it does the job of a storage system, just like a regular wallet. For a wallet I recommend Metamask and Trustwallet. You'll learn more about all of these in the following chapters.

CoinGecko

Operating since 2014, CoinGecko is one of the most popular websites for live (real-time) cryptocurrency price listings. At the same time, CoinGecko welcomes new cryptocurrency users to the community with educational materials, performance profit calculations, and interactive giveaways. Upon entering CoinGecko, we see Bitcoin on the homepage as the top cryptocurrency with the largest market cap and largest network. However, there are thousands of currencies out there for you to discover. CoinGecko has categorized all the different token features to allow users to see a plethora of different data and information related to cryptocurrency markets.

OKX Exchange

OKX, launched in 2017 is a Seychelles-based crypto powerhouse, unites millions of users worldwide. It offers a comprehensive range of services, including spot and options trading, derivatives, trading bots, savings, DeFi, and more. Their wallet, known as the "portal to Web3," includes a DEX, NFT marketplace, and DApps, supporting over 30 networks. OKX also boasts its native blockchain, OKX Chain, and the OKB token for developers and DApp enthusiasts.

Binance Exchange

Binance Exchange is a leading cryptocurrency exchange founded in 2017 in China. It has a strong focus on altcoin trading. It offers cryptocurrency-to-cryptocurrency trading in more than 500 cryptocurrencies and virtual tokens, including Bitcoin (BTC), Ether (ETH), Litecoin (LTC), Dogecoin (DOGE), and its own token, Binance Coin (BNB). Later, it moved its headquarters out of China following the Chinese government's increasing regulation of cryptocurrency.

Trust Wallet

It is a decentralized wallet, controlled by the user, where the user holds the keys to the cryptocurrency wallet. A wallet in which only the user is in control of his or her funds, has access to DApps, and does not store personal information, unlike centralized wallets. Its main goal is to make crypto more accessible.

MetaMask

MetaMask is a cryptocurrency wallet software used to interact with the Ethereum blockchain. It allows users to access the wallet where they hold Ethereum through a browser extension or mobile app, which can then be used to interact with decentralized applications. MetaMask has been developed by

ConsenSys Software Inc, a blockchain software company focused on Ethereum-based tools and infrastructure.

MetaMask allows users to store and manage account keys, transmit transactions, send and receive Ethereum-based cryptocurrencies and tokens, and securely connect to decentralized applications via a compatible web browser or the app's built-in mobile browser.

How to Buy Cryptocurrencies?

If you are new to the world of cryptocurrencies, learning how to buy Bitcoin, Dogecoin, Ethereum, and other cryptocurrencies can be confusing at first. In this book, I'll show you step-by-step how to do it.

You can start investing in cryptocurrencies by following the five easy steps outlined below. Alternatively, you can go to my YouTube channel and, with the help of one of my videos, make your initial registration and your first investments in an exchange. In the videos on my channel, I show you step-by-step what you need to do. Here, I list the basics you need to do for your first purchases.

1. Choose a platform or exchange

   To buy cryptocurrencies, you must first choose a cryptocurrency exchange.

What is a cryptocurrency exchange?

A cryptocurrency exchange is a platform where buyers and sellers meet to exchange cryptocurrencies. Exchanges often have relatively low fees, but tend to have more complex user interfaces (UI) with multiple transaction types and advanced performance graphs. This can be daunting for new cryptocurrency investors.

Some of the most well-known cryptocurrency exchanges are Binance, Coinbase, and Gemini. While the standard trading interfaces of these companies can overwhelm beginners, especially those without a trading history, they still offer easy shopping options that are user-friendly.

However, convenience comes at a cost, as beginner-friendly options charge significantly more than it would cost to buy cryptocurrency through each platform's standard trading interface. If you want it to cost you less, you can learn how to use the standard trading platforms before you make your first cryptocurrency purchase.

An important note: As a new cryptocurrency user, you should make sure that the exchange you have chosen allows fiat currency transfers (currencies such as the dollar or the euro). Some exchanges only allow you to buy cryptocurrencies using other cryptocurrencies. This means that you will need to find another exchange to buy tokens accepted by the exchange of your choice before you can start trading cryptocurrencies on that platform.

2. Create and verify your account

   Once you have selected a cryptocurrency exchange, you can register to open an account. Depending on the platform and the amount you intend to invest, you will usually need to verify your identity. The platform may ask you to submit a copy of your ID card, driver's license, or passport. It may even ask you to upload a selfie (a photo of yourself) to prove that your appearance matches the documents you submitted.

This is now one of the standard steps to open an account at a cryptocurrency exchange such as Binance, etc. Only decentralized exchanges do not require data identification.

It's not a difficult step, but it's the step where most people give up because they fail to send the right photos, or they're afraid something bad will happen to them if someone has their information, or simply because they don't understand what to do. So they give up altogether because they don't have the patience to submit the information.

It's really very simple. At each step, the platform will ask you for a photo or some information from a document certifying your identity or address. You fill in the details and send a good photo of your ID (or other authentication document) as it asks. Then all the next steps will be done automatically and you will have access to your account and the exchange options.

3. Cash deposit for investment

This is also a simple step. To buy cryptocurrencies, you will need to put money into your account after you have chosen your central exchange (e.g., Binance). There, you will link your bank account and authorize a wire transfer or make a payment with a debit or credit card.

With a card from your bank or a bank transfer, you can make the payment, so you can then buy the cryptocurrency of your choice. Then you can actually buy the cryptocurrencies you want or simply select the quantity of a cryptocurrency.

There is no longer a problem with banks when it comes to buying cryptocurrencies. It would just be a good idea to do this the first time with one of the largest and most well-known exchanges so there is familiarity with the process as well as security. It's easy enough, and this will be your first cryptocurrency investment.

4. Buy the cryptocurrency you want

Now, you just buy the cryptocurrency you want. When you decide which cryptocurrency to buy, you can enter its symbol (e.g., for Bitcoin it's BTC and for Ethereum it's ETH).

This is the step where you really make your investment. You can also buy a stablecoin, such as USDT, which will retain the same value as the money you put in at the beginning, neither going up nor down. You can do this if you don't want to invest directly in a cryptocurrency because the timing might not be right. But at the same time, you want to have your money in the exchange, ready and available to buy the cryptocurrency of your choice at the time you think is most appropriate.

Whatever your decision is, the exchange is really like a bank account, which simply gives you the option to hold your money in different cryptocurrencies. To gain access, simply connect your regular bank account, put a sum of money into the exchange, and you can start exchanging cryptocurrencies.

Usually, when you first sign up on a platform, the platform itself will guide you through all the steps to get you to buy your first cryptocurrencies. From there, you can exchange them for other cryptocurrencies or send them to other exchanges and decentralized exchanges.

5. Choose a storage method

    The last step has to do with where you decide to store your cryptocurrency. One can keep one's cryptocurrency in an exchange or send it to another wallet where one intends to keep it for a long time and have more security.

You can leave your cryptocurrency on the exchange itself initially. When you buy some cryptocurrency, it is usually stored on the exchange. If you don't like your exchange, you can transfer them to another one. In general, most large exchanges now have enough security systems and good customer service to help you if something happens to your account. It's not easy to pull a trick and have a theft through the exchanges if you haven't given access to a third party. In the event that the exchange itself has a problem, they will compensate you, as many of the major exchanges now have security accounts for this kind of hacking damage, which they use to compensate victims.

You can also keep them in a cold wallet. Cryptocurrency cold wallets are not connected to the internet, which makes them the safest option for storing cryptocurrency. They come in the form of external devices, such as a USB drive or a hard drive. You can simply send your cryptocurrency to such a hard drive and rest assured that no one can steal it over the internet, unless your hard drive or USB is stolen.

However, you should be careful with cold wallets, because if you lose the key code associated with them or the device is damaged, you may never be able to recover your cryptocurrency.

What Is a Cryptocurrency Broker?

Cryptocurrency brokers take the complexity out of the cryptocurrency market by offering easy-to-use interfaces that interact with exchanges on your behalf. Some charge more than the exchanges. Others claim they are "free" while making money by selling information to large brokerages or mutual funds about what you and other traders are buying and selling. They may also not execute your trades at the best possible market price. Robinhood and SoFi are two of the most well-known cryptocurrency brokers.

Although they are undoubtedly convenient to use, you should be careful with brokers because you may face restrictions on moving your cryptocurrency holdings off-platform. At Robinhood and SoFi, for example, you cannot move cryptocurrencies outside of your account. This may not seem like a huge problem, but advanced cryptocurrency investors prefer to keep their coins in cryptocurrency wallets for extra security. Some even opt for hardware cryptocurrency wallets that are not connected to the internet for even more security.

What Are NFTs?

Non-Fungible Tokens (NFTs) are digitally encrypted assets that do not have the property of being fungible. They can be associated either with any digital artwork file, such as photos, videos, sounds, and other types of multimedia, or with a digital representation of a physical object.

They contain identifying information about their holders, recorded in smart contracts. This information makes each NFT truly unique, as it cannot be replaced by another token. It is easily verifiable and the original issuer can be traced without difficulty. Thus, each NFT is considered to have certificates of originality. An NFT can be anything, such as a photograph, a song, or a video. The value of an NFT comes from its rarity, just like a really good work of art. It also has the potential to appreciate more over time.

Usually, investors buy them for the value they will have in the future. Artists prefer to make their works on NFTs because they can make more profits and their artworks can never be stolen or copied, as their data and creation information will always be stored on the blockchain.

What Determines the Value of an NFT

NFTs derive value from 4 key elements:

- Rarity: The rarity of an NFT determines its value and has the potential to appreciate in value more over time.

- Collectability: Like baseball cards, artwork and antiques, NFTs are popular digital collectibles that offer a unique niche for collectors.
- Supply utility: Some types of NFTs provide utility, such as objects or items in a game (avatars, weapons, trinkets) and even virtual real estate.
- Investment: NFTs are the "craze" of the digital economy, offering money-making opportunities when traded.

How to Buy an NFT

These digital assets have seen growth in trading through the use of cryptocurrencies such as Bitcoin or Ethereum. Most users buy NFTs in exclusive markets, similar to how they would buy cryptocurrencies. There are millions of Non-Fungible Tokens in the various NFT markets. You just need to learn how to buy NFTs.

Although the NFT market is relatively new, buying your first digital collectible is not difficult in terms of ease of use.

Below is a step-by-step guide to a simple purchase of an NFT.

1. Wallet setting

    To buy an NFT, you must first buy some cryptocurrency and link it to your cryptocurrency wallet. You can buy cryptocurrencies such as Bitcoin, BNB, and Ethereum. Your digital wallet is where you keep your cryptocurrency – a place to send or receive it – and your money to buy cryptocurrency apps and services. Once you have created and funded your digital wallet, then buying an NFT becomes an easy process. Later, when you collect a few NFTs, they will be stored in your Metamask wallet or another digital wallet. There are many digital wallets, such as the Binance wallet, the Ethereum network, and several others.

2. Select a Marketplace for NFTs

   After setting up your digital wallet, you will need to select a Marketplace to purchase your NFTs. There are many leading NFT Marketplaces such as OpenSea, Rarible, Mintable, Axie Marketplace, Binance, and *Crypto.com*, that sell NFTs. Most Marketplaces offer the sale of digital art, music, collectibles, virtual items, in-game items, and more. These Marketplaces usually make it easy for users to create, sell, and buy NFTs. However, before you start buying, you need to learn how to avoid NFT scams.

3. Connect your digital wallet to the Marketplace

   Once you have selected the NFT Marketplace you want, you then need to link it to your cryptocurrency wallet. OpenSea is considered the largest NFT Marketplace, allowing users to interact and exchange NFTs from many different Marketplaces and blockchains. Once logged into a Marketplace, you can buy, sell, and exchange NFTs. If you choose platforms like Binance and *Crypto.com*, you don't need to do anything else after purchasing because the NFTs will be stored directly in your account, which you have already created when you joined their app. The technology is running and it all becomes much easier and handy.

4. Find an NFT you like

   In the list of items offered for sale in the Marketplace of your choice, select the NFTs you like. Remember that to buy NFTs you should choose those that are popular, going viral, or are rare in order to attract higher prices in the future. To do this successfully, you need to learn the basics, such as how to find successful social media projects, how to see the potential value of a project, and various other things we will see below.

5. Submit an offer or purchase

   Once you have decided on the NFT you want to buy, you can start the purchase by submitting an offer on the NFT or by paying the price the seller is asking. NFT sellers provide potential buyers with details about the buying process, such as the selling price of the NFT, the auction time limit, and the cryptocurrencies they will accept from buyers.

6. Complete the Transaction

   If your bid for the NFT is the highest at the end of the auction, then the purchase of the NFT will be automatically completed. If the NFT is not in an auction, then at the moment you pay you will buy it automatically and it will appear after a few seconds or minutes in your wallet.

7. Retention or sale of the NFT

   You hold your NFT until it reaches a price that can bring you a profit if you sell it. Alternatively, you can save it as part of your unique personal collection if you simply wish to have it.

NFT Buying Tips

The best way to decide on an NFT purchase is to consider the following:

Find the type of NFTs you are looking for. Not all NFTs have the same value. Some are highly sought after, while others are popular in niche markets. There are artworks that you want for a personal collection and there are others that will increase in value in the future. The purchase of an NFT will be determined by what you want to do with it. Is it for your personal needs as a collector or fan? Or do you want to make money from it when it goes up in price?

See the charges of the NFT Marketplace. NFT purchases come with commissions and fees, the so-called "gas fees," which vary from Marketplace to Marketplace. "Gas fees" are payments made by users to compensate for the computational energy required to process and validate transactions. On the

Ethereum blockchain the "gas fees" are quite high, while on the Binance smart chain they are very, very low (at the time of writing).

Is the Marketplace user-friendly? If you are new to NFT trading, make sure that the processes and user interface are easy to use and simple to facilitate your shopping experience. A Marketplace like Binance can be best for a new buyer before moving on to something more complicated.

How Do You Know What NFTs to Buy?

Depending on the purpose of your purchase, you will determine what type of NFTs you would like to buy. If you're a collector or fan, you can choose to buy memorabilia, sports cards, digital artwork, and more that align with your passion. If you want to invest in NFTs, look for NFTs that will have good prices in the future. The best bet is to go by popularity, hype, how viral a collection is, and of course, rarity to get good returns on your investment in the future.

Of course, just as you can buy, you can also resell an NFT, just like anything else you own. Simply, to resell your NFT, you need to make sure that the NFT is in the cryptocurrency wallet associated with the Marketplace in which you want to sell it. I mention this because many times, when someone opens multiple accounts and wallets, they can get confused and think they have lost an asset when they simply have it in another e-wallet.

Finally, Why Do People Buy Digital Art on NFTs?

The digital art trade, like NFTs, is the "craze" that is fueling the digital economy right now. Today, NFTs have helped create a marketplace for digital art where users can safely create an NFT, store it, buy it, sell it, and collect it. Artists have an interest in giving their work as an NFT because it solves all their problems. In this way, NFTs overcome the problem of authenticity, since once such a work is made, it will forever bear the signature of that particular artist.

In addition, NFT blockchains help NFT creators track all transactions after their initial sale, allowing for ongoing royalty payments, helping them to have a steady revenue stream. That is, the creator of an NFT can receive a percentage, for example 10%, from each sale of that project in the future. This is a powerful incentive, so the artists themselves have an interest in raising the price and making their NFTs worth even more in the future. That's why we see more well-known artists joining the NFT market every week.

How to Create and Sell an NFT

First you will need to create or more formally "mint" your NFT. To create an NFT for your artwork, you need to choose an NFT platform and a payment wallet. You will use the wallet to pay the gas fees, as well as to receive payments when you sell some NFTs.

There are many online platforms that you can use to create and sell an NFT. Some of the most popular NFT auction platforms are OpenSea, Rarible, SuperRare, Foundation, VIV3, Nifty Gateway, Axie Marketplace, NFT ShowRoom, and BakerySwap. There are also other NFT platforms, and new ones are opening all the time. On many exchanges you can also buy and sell NFTs with much simpler procedures.

There are many NFT payment platforms, such as MetaMask. For illustrative purposes, we will go through the process required to create and sell an NFT using one of the above platforms and your MetaMask wallet.

Whichever platform you choose, you will follow a similar process. On exchanges, the process is much simpler, because you don't have to make complicated transactions and links to different wallets, since your account contains your wallet from the start.

Here are the steps to create and sell an NFT.

1. Buy some cryptocurrency to fund your wallet

   Most NFT platforms use the cryptocurrency Ethereum, because the first big projects started with it. All of the NFT auction platforms listed above are paid upfront to mint an NFT. Minting an NFT is the process of turning a work of art into an NFT that can be sold. So initially, you need to have a quantity of cryptocurrency in your account. Here I should tell you that it is not a process that costs a few cents of the dollar or anything like that. The cost of minting an NFT can start from tens of dollars and go up to thousands.

ETH is the most commonly accepted currency, as it is the native cryptocurrency of the open-source blockchain platform Ethereum, where NFTs were first released. However, some platforms are starting to accept a variety of payment formats and create NFTs using different blockchains.

If you don't already have some ETH, there are many cryptocurrency exchanges where you can buy ETH or other currencies. The quickest and easiest option, however, is to buy ETH directly with your digital wallet.

2. Create a digital wallet to pay for your NFT

   To create a digital wallet with MetaMask, you need to go to its website and click on the "Download" button on the top right. If you are using a desktop computer, you will be prompted to install the browser extension. There is also a mobile app.

You will be asked to confirm that you wish to "create a new wallet and seed phrase." You do not need to worry about what "seed phrase" means. It's just a list of words that stores information about the blockchain. Say "Yes," review the terms, and if you agree, then accept them. Create a password, follow some security steps, and finally, you're ready to set up your account.

The terminology that exists in the cryptocurrency world can make this part of learning how to create and sell an NFT quite daunting, but the process is actually very easy.

3. Connect your wallet to an NFT platform

    Most digital wallets work in a similar way. Whichever one you choose, you will need to connect it to the NFT platform you will use to sell the NFT. There are many NFT platforms to choose from, and the process is generally similar to the one described below. Go to the platform you have chosen and click "Connect wallet."

4. Upload the file you want to convert to NFT

    At this stage you will have a wallet linked to ETH to make the payment. You are now ready to upload an NFT. You will be given options to create a single project or sell the same item multiple times. There you need to upload the digital file you want to convert to an NFT. The platforms usually accept files such as PNG, GIF, MP4, and MP3.

5. Organizing an auction for your NFT

    The next stage is to choose how to sell your NFT. There are three options. "Fixed Price" allows you to set a price and sell your NFT at that price when a buyer is found. The "Unlimited Auction" option allows users to continue to submit bids until you accept one of them. Finally, the "Timed Auction" is an auction that only lasts for a set amount of time and the bidder buys the NFT when the time expires.

This leads us to the most difficult part: choosing the price, or at least the minimum price. If you sell your NFT too cheaply, the huge gas fees for this whole process will reduce your profits and you may end up paying out of pocket.

6. Preparation before selling your NFT

    Now you can add a title and description for your NFT. To maximize the chance of your NFT selling at a high price, you should put some time and imagination into this step. You will then be asked to consider the percentage of royalties you want to claim in any future resale of your art. This is a good place to get passive income in the future. For any resale of your work by its future owners, you will receive a percentage, say 20%, of the net sale value of the work.

On the other hand, while in the long run a higher rate will make you more money per sale, to some extent it will deter others from reselling your art because they will be less likely to make a large profit for themselves.

Finally, there is an optional field to add the properties of your file.

7. Payment of the registration fee for your NFT

    The last step is to click on "Create Listing" where you will be asked to log in with your wallet to pay the registration fee for your NFT.

This is where the charges start. The registration fee may be low, e.g., 5 dollars, but to go further, you will have to agree to an additional fee to actually create your NFT, which can be equivalent to, for example, 50 dollars in ETH. Later, when someone buys your NFT, you'll have to pay a commission for selling the NFT, plus a transaction fee for transferring the money from the buyer's wallet to yours. All together it's a large amount, which changes depending on what phase the cryptocurrency market is generally in at the time.

I would like to explain in a simple and clear way how to calculate the potential cost of creating and selling an NFT, but the confusing nature of blockchain technology, the wild fluctuations in cryptocurrency prices, and the lack of transparency on the platforms themselves, make it almost impossible. This is where experience and trial and error come into play. You have to take the risk, wait to see how much you will be charged in total for a sale, and hope you make a profit. Testing in this area costs quite a bit, but it can also bring in a lot of revenue.

What Is Minting?

As with physical currency, "minting" is the term used for the process of creating currency and NFTs on a blockchain. With NFTs, it is usually on Ethereum. The minting process records data in a public ledger that is immutable and unalterable, which can track and monitor the NFTs as future sales are made. Minting usually has a cost – the "gas fee" mentioned above. Depending on the Marketplace, how, when, and to whom the fees are charged changes, so it requires personal study.

Any kind of digital file can be stored and become an NFT. Marketplaces have been created for digital artworks such as videos, game assets, and music. Physical objects are now being digitized as NFTs, for example, limited edition clothing, usually jerseys from football teams and players. In the future, there will be NFTs between the digital and physical space.

Why Are NFTs so Popular?

The Popularity of NFTs

Most people who start researching NFTs for the first time may be confused by the big hype and very little data about them. In fact, it's a very easy subject. Someone can make a piece of artwork and sell it on a platform to make money from it. Someone else just buys that artwork in various ways. Basically, it's as simple as buying a cryptocurrency and later on he can do whatever he wants with what he bought. Many people buy NFTs to resell them in the future for greater profit.

After reading various articles about the prices of these works, you will begin to understand why these works are not just some useless JPEG files. There are people who will easily pay anywhere from a few thousand to hundreds of thousands of dollars for a single image.

This new digital encryption collectibles sector is changing not only the future of art collecting, but also the future of digital ownership.

NFT is an abbreviation of Non-Fungible Token. If an item is exchangeable, its value is what defines it – not its unique properties. For example, a dollar is exchangeable because it can be exchanged for any other dollar and retain the same value. Corn, oil, and gold are all exchangeable because the commodities can be directly exchanged. Similarly, most cryptocurrencies are exchangeable because each unit has the same value.

Without a doubt, Twitter is the first place to look when delving into the world of NFTs. The NFT community is highly active on Twitter, making it one of the best places to learn about upcoming projects, explore its communities, and get updates on specific projects.

You can easily find new projects on Twitter using #NFT, #NFTCommunity, and #cryptoart. Following NFT-related accounts will help you understand the NFT field better.

Discord is also a critical platform for NFT projects, but it's not necessarily the most user-friendly. Discord allows users to delve into various projects and communicate with other members about those projects. It features private invitation-only groups, which are often only accessible by purchasing an NFT.

CryptoPunks was the first major NFT project and was launched in 2021. Only CryptoPunks members can chat in the group they have on Discord, but reading the discussions will provide excellent insight. The discussion will educate you on how they think about and analyze new projects, projects that attract interest in the Punk market, and how experienced NFT traders operate.

The Bored Ape Yacht Club group on Discord is also worth following for its announcements. The creators discuss what they have done to add value to the project and how it has evolved into a brand name. The conversation on Discord is very active and encourages members to participate, ask questions, and seek help from industry professionals.

These platforms are particularly useful to find projects that will have more value in the future and thus make a good investment.

Let's now look at some Marketplaces for NFTs.

OpenSea is the world's first and largest NFT Marketplace. It is the most important platform for trading, selling, and project creation on Web3. Other benefits of browsing the platform include using it to learn more about the market and new NFT projects, as well as to keep track of trends.

With so many NFT projects available, it's like being in a minefield and trying to guess which one will succeed and which one will fail. How can one tell the difference between the NFT projects that will thrive and those that will fail?

Well, the short answer is research. When investing in anything, one must first learn about the subject (and ideally become an expert on it). It takes a while to identify solid projects in the NFT market, but the chances of finding proper projects increase significantly with some extra work.

One of the things to consider includes the attraction of the project. On this issue, you will find reliable information on Discord or from influencers on Twitter. As a rule, having over 10,000 followers on Twitter and Discord is a sign of a good project. Of course, this is only true if the followers are real.

The team behind the NFT is also an important element. Who is the creator? Who is investing in the project? Do they have a meaningful purpose with the project?

Finally, the number of sales and price fluctuations in recent days or weeks should be taken into account.

Together, all these factors can give a good indication of whether an NFT will fail or fly!

Some Good NFTs

In general, there are a lot of NFTs now and all exchanges more or less have put up corresponding options for people to work and invest in. Exchanges like Binance and *Crypto.com* promote them heavily and daily provide new options with NFT-related actions.

NTFs are the new trend in the financial and economic markets. It is the part of the cryptocurrency market that is revolutionizing finance and art at the same time. Cryptocurrency fanatics have so far thought of a thousand ways to invest in art, music, and sports with the help of NFTs.

While Cardano, Solana, and other blockchains are becoming more and more popular, Ethereum is establishing itself as the big opportunity in the NFT world.

NFTs were made famous through the Ethereum chain, and so we're going to look at some promising Ethereum NFTs that are making huge strides in the financial markets. Amid investor speculation about delays in the ETH 2.0 upgrade, Ethereum NFTs are stealing the spotlight from this controversy.

Here are some of the most well-known and large NFT projects that are currently being released.

Axie Infinity

Axie Infinity is known in the NFT market as one of the most popular NFT games and a lucrative cryptocurrency. The game was released in 2018 and has gained almost 2 million players from all over the world. Axie Infinity is a popular Ethereum NFT project that allows players to enter a battle game where players can train and grow creatures like Axies.

Decentraland

Decentraland is a virtual web space that is three-dimensional. The platform is built on the Ethereum blockchain and has made huge strides since its launch in 2020. It allows players to buy plots using the internal cryptocurrency MANA. Players can buy land, explore Decentraland, and take full control of the platform through smart contracts.

CryptoPunks

The CryptoPunks project was created in 2017 and is one of the first and most successful Ethereum NFT projects on the market. Each of the punks is created algorithmically, but the collectibles are limited to 10,000 punks. Human Punks are the most popular among investors, but there are other types as well. Of course, prices are several thousand dollars for each of these NFTs.

Gods Unchained

Gods Unchained is also one of the biggest Ethereum NFT projects that have been a huge success in the last year. The NFT game is free for players who wish to complete the ownership of their in-game assets. Gods Unchained is a deck building game in which players can collect, build, and sell cards.

The Sandbox

The Sandbox is another popular NFT project, known mainly for its virtual world and blockchain-based video game. It is a community-based virtual conversion game that allows creators to generate revenue from assets and games on the blockchain system.

NBA TopShot

NBA TopShot is a marketplace that enables NBA fans to trade NFTs of "NBA Moments." NBA stands for "National Basketball Association," which is the governing body of the basketball league of the same name in the USA. "NBA Moments" are highlights of NBA games, consisting of video clips. NBA TopShot is quite popular among NBA fanatics. NBA TopShot was named one of the most important Ethereum NFT projects of 2021 for its role in enabling widespread adoption and awareness about NFTs.

Bored Ape Yacht Club

The Bored Ape NFT collection is one of the most popular and also the most controversial NFT projects in the industry. Since their release, Bored Apes have skyrocketed in value, and some of these NFTs are worth millions. The collection managed to surpass the value of CryptoPunks, impressing the cryptocurrency and NFT industry.

Remarkable Women

The Remarkable Women NFT project is a tribute to strong women who chose to believe in collective power and accelerated a cultural transformation. These NTFs are the creation of Rachel Winter, a renowned Canadian illustrator. Winter's background in fashion and the arts and her experience in pattern design have made these NTFs the perfect combination of culture and feminism.

Cyber Cosmos World

Cyber Cosmos World is ready to make its mark on the metaverse to promote women's empowerment. The NFT project consists of 10,000 avatars, the Cyber Warriors, representing women in the tech industry. The project is based on the Ethereum blockchain.

CryptoKitties

CryptoKitties is another popular Ethereum NFT project that uses blockchain technology in games. The project is incredibly popular and one of the best Ethereum NFT projects available. The game involves playing, collecting, and managing virtual NFTs for cats.

These were 10 important NFT projects. There are many more options out there, and one has to do a lot of research to find out which ones are worth investing in. Of course, one must also watch out for potential scams.

Bull Market and Bear Market

What Is a Bull Market?

A "Bull Market" is a name for an uptrending market, characterized by an increase in the value of stocks. It occurs when asset prices in a market rise steadily over time. When describing assets such as cryptocurrencies, stocks, commodities, and bonds, the phrase "Bull Market" is widely used. It can also be used for other types of investments, such as real estate. During an uptrending market, investors acquire a large number of stocks with the expectation that their value will increase and that they can make a profit by selling them later. It is not just a trend for a few days, but something that lasts for several weeks. In the stock market they say that if a market goes up for at least 2 months, then it is definitely a Bull Market.

How Does the Bull Market Work?

In determining a Bull Market, no specific benchmark or standard applies. The most important indicator is a continuous period of rising currency price in the market. Bull markets are characterized by investor growth, optimism, confidence, and other positive characteristics. It is a period when the prices of major assets are expected to rise for a long period of time.

Bull markets are difficult to predict, but they are easy to spot when prices rise by 20% or more. The most recent bull market in cryptocurrencies was in May 2020 and lasted for at least 1 year before the first signs of a decline appeared in the summer of 2021. Around February 2022 was the time when the cryptocurrency market had fallen enough. So, we were talking then about the end of the Bull Market era for cryptocurrencies.

How Long Does It Take to End a Bull Market?

"What goes up must come down," as the saying goes. While many investors are buying and holding on to their investments, they expect the bull market to continue indefinitely. However, the stock market will always go through boom-and-bust phases due to the business cycle.

It is worth noting that there are as many uptrending markets as there are downtrending markets, otherwise known as "Bear Markets," despite the fact that bull markets often last much longer. In fact, the longest bull market in the history of the stock market lasted more than ten years. Cryptocurrencies go in cycles that last up to two years, although generally the whole idea of cryptocurrencies is very new. So if you're scared about what's going to happen if we enter a down market, fear not. History teaches that down markets are only temporary. Also, a down market is the best place to buy and accumulate assets, while a rising market is the best place to sell.

Characteristics of a Bull Market

- Booming markets are often associated with growing economies, so a characteristic is a booming economy. Unemployment is also falling, while corporate profits are rising.
- Optimism and confidence. Investors are more confident and optimistic about their purchases, which encourages them to buy, and thus prices rise even more.
- There is a great willingness by investors to acquire assets rather than dispose of them.

Bullish markets can be assessed in terms of increased employment and corporate profits. They are also characterized by a lack of supply and high demand.

Bullish markets are the polar opposites of bearish markets. Both have a huge influence on global financial markets, positive in bull markets and negative in bear markets.

Bear Markets are associated with price falls and excessive pessimism, while Bull Markets are associated with price rises and confidence in the financial market. Bullish markets indicate economic and financial expansion. Investors who understand how to take advantage of bull markets are the ones who profit the most.

Bull Run

A Bull Run (also known as an uptrend) is a period of time in the financial market during which the values of certain assets are constantly rising. We usually use this term for an asset and its uptrend, whereas the term Bull Market indicates that the entire market is on the rise. An asset can even have a Bull Run in a Bear Market, where everything goes down in that particular market and this asset goes up.

During the uptrend of a cryptocurrency, the value of this asset is constantly increasing. At this point, investors show a strong interest in this asset, thus increasing the demand for it.

Finally, the demand for the aforementioned cryptocurrency asset outstrips the supply, indicating an optimistic mood among cryptocurrency investors.

Similarly, when the price of a cryptocurrency asset continues to increase on a steady basis, it indicates that the cryptocurrency is trending upwards. The process that drives the values of a cryptocurrency asset is closely linked to the attitude of the investors involved in the process.

Although the duration of a Bull Run can vary, to be recognized as a Bull Run, it must normally last for an extended period of time. It can last for several months or even years. The cryptocurrency market is very new, so these rules are mostly derived from those that apply to stocks.

The reasons for creating a Bull Run can also vary. Prices can rise over a long period of time as a result of variables such as investor optimism and confidence, among others. However, the halving of Bitcoin (cutting the reward for mining Bitcoin in half) is usually a trigger for these Bull Runs in a cryptocurrency market. This means that whenever Bitcoin reaches a point where it becomes more difficult to mine, then its value starts to rise and is sustained for several months. Of course, when Bitcoin goes up or down, it pulls all other currencies with it, either up or down.

As we have seen above, a Bull Market is a term used to describe a market that is experiencing an uptrend. A Bull Market is the polar opposite of a Bear Market, where asset values tend to fall for a long period of time, perhaps due to pessimism.

Similarly, investors can be considered "bullish" on an asset or market if they believe it will rise in value, or "bearish" if they believe it will fall in value.

For example, in January 2017, the price of Bitcoin surpassed $1,100 and this was the highest record price to date. Within a few months, the price rose to around $20,000 per coin. In other words, an increase of about 19 times in less than a year.

The price increase in 2017 occurred a year after Bitcoin halving, and something similar had happened before, in 2013. One of the characteristics of this period was that, for the first time, the general public became interested in cryptocurrencies. The mainstream media started to cover articles about Bitcoin. This price increase was mainly due to retail investors entering the market for the first time.

Bear Trend and Bear Market

A Bear Trend is the downward trend of an asset. Bear Market we have when the entire market has this trend. There is no agreed rule for when a bear trend occurs, but the commonly accepted definition is that it occurs when the market has retreated more than 20% from its previous highs.

All of these terms exist in investments, but there is no statistical standard or rule for when one or the other applies. That's what makes it interesting, as all the experts make up their own rules, where some get it right and some get it wrong. After something like this, the public will follow those who are more correct, judging by the result.

As for the Bear Market, when it continues, investors continue to fear that they will lose money and sell their assets. Many people see Bear Market trends as an opportunity to make money due to low asset prices, but this involves finding an appropriate entry point into the market. Finding a suitable entry point is not the easiest thing. Unlike a Bull Market, in which almost anywhere you enter you will make a profit, in a Bear Market if you enter at the wrong point, you can lose a lot. In some cases, especially in a market like cryptocurrencies which is very new, you can lose it all.

While "Bear" is the definition for a person who is cautious or pessimistic, the related term "Bear Market" describes a market that has experienced significant downward pressure over a prolonged period of time.

In a Bear Market, traders and new investors are more likely to sell than to buy. A famous Bear Trend was the 410-day decline in Bitcoin, which occurred between 2013 and 2015. There are many possible reasons why a bear trend can be created, and these can vary significantly depending on the currency or token.

Mainstream financial commentators and many institutional investors are extremely honest in their bearish predictions for cryptocurrencies. Despite the huge gains seen in many digital currencies over the years, many of these individuals (aka Bears) argue that the momentum of cryptocurrencies is not sustainable.

There are several rules among dedicated cryptocurrency traders in this regard, and indeed, a bearish outlook may accompany certain events. In Bitcoin, for example, Bear Trends tend to precede halvings, which in turn tend to trigger a Bull Market, i.e., a period of consecutive Bull Run.

An important fact is that Bear Markets should not be confused with price corrections or Pullbacks (temporary pause or small drop in the price of an asset or security that is in an uptrend). A price correction refers to a decrease in the price of an asset or security of more than 10% compared to its most recent high. A price correction may cause a market decline or may be short-lived. But it occurs for exactly the reason its name implies, to correct the price of an asset. In theory, if the price of Bitcoin goes up a lot, it would have to go down a little to reach what is considered its true value.

For example, if it now went from $40,000 to $50,000 in a few days, it would be reasonable that it would then drop for a few days to about $45,000. That would just be a price correction and would have nothing to do with the Bear theories. Something like this shows that an asset, due to excitement or other such factors, can go up more than its true value for a short period of time and then fall back down to what the market believes is its true value for that period.

A Bear Market is usually created by an economic downturn or a major event that occurs, such as the Ukraine-Russia war or the global lockdown, which has a large negative impact on the economy.

Some speculate that the term "Bear Market" is named after an old saying that you don't sell the bear skin before you catch the bear. Others believe the term is named after the way a bear attacks its prey by dragging its feet downward, while a bull attacks upward. With these symbolisms they differentiate a bearish market from a bullish one.

The fact is that Bear Markets do occur from time to time. Since World War II, Wall Street has officially had at least 13 Bear Markets (every five or six years on average), each lasting about a year.

A Bear Market usually corrects itself and the economy recovers fairly quickly. However, if asset values continue to fall, a recession may be triggered. When the economy stops expanding for a long period of time – usually two or more quarters of negative economic growth – there is what is known as a recession.

A Pullback is a 5% to 10% price reduction that is only temporary and generally lasts for a few days or weeks. It is like going through a period of adjustment, making a small detour from a recent price high, but with no change in the existing trend.

A market correction occurs when prices fall by 10% to 20%. It lasts in this zone for up to four months or so. These periods are highly volatile. They can cause investors to fear that a Bear Market will occur and therefore sell. Real-time news can exacerbate these concerns, as investors may be influenced by crowd psychology and take preemptive action. The summer of 2021 was one such period. Then, from the autumn onwards, we saw the market set new records again.

A Bear Market occurs when prices fall by 20% or more and can last from months to years. Investor confidence suffers and most investors exit the market. More and more investors sell their assets to avoid further losses, and trading activity declines across the industry.

Now, of course, these percentages are for traditional markets and are derived from stock market theories, while they do not apply to cryptocurrencies. In cryptocurrencies an asset can go up or down more than 20% in a few hours or a few days. We often see some cryptocurrencies rise more than 100 times in value in a matter of days or weeks. In fact, this is one of the reasons why many young people enter this market: to take advantage of such an opportunity and make a lot of money.

During Bear Markets, various bubbles also appear in the market, such as the related Dot-Com bubble that lasted from 2000 to 2002. When it burst, the cost of the loss to investors was $5 trillion! The late 1990s was a period of rapid expansion for many new technology companies such as Google, Amazon, and Yahoo! as widespread use of the internet fueled market expansion. The S&P 500 index (Standard & Poor's 500) rose nearly 400% before plummeting 49% in March 2000.

Prices were driven so high by excessive speculation and positive market enthusiasm that they could no longer be justified. They had far exceeded the real value of each share. As investors continued to pour money into Dot-Com shares, supply began to outstrip demand. More and more companies wanted to go public, sometimes without a good plan, and managed to attract investors in non-productive activities. This, of course, blew up somewhere and then it all went down the drain.

In terms of cryptocurrencies, for example, in December 2017, Bitcoin went from around $20,000 to just over $3,200 in a few days, making it one of the most well-known faults in the cryptocurrency world. After that, the price rose again, reaching around $65,000 per coin in April 2021, before plummeting to below $32,000 in May of that year.

A year later, the currency fell below $20,000 and found itself in a bear market. This pulled all other cryptocurrencies down. So we can say that to some extent, whatever bubble there was burst, as by early 2022 many cryptocurrency projects that had no product or good plan were forced to close or declare bankruptcy. Among these were the leading projects Celsius and Luna, along with the UST stablecoin. These created even more fear throughout the market, which is the hallmark of a Bear Market. A Bear Market has enough of these events to scare investors even more.

There is also the term Bear Trap, which actually means a trap. It involves a number of traders who have significant amounts of cryptocurrencies in their possession. Together, they will arrange to sell a large amount of that currency at the same time, with the intention of convincing other market participants that a price correction is taking place, so that they will sell their assets and thus prices will fall even further. At this point they will fall into the Bear Trap and the group of traders will buy back their assets at a lower price. The value of the currency will then recover, and those who set the trap will reap profits.

The term Bear Trap came from the stock market, like all the terms we saw so far. However, in this context, the term is used to describe both the technique used and the specific indicator of reversing a downward trend in the market. Of course, this is illegal, but it happens anyway, especially in the cryptocurrency market, where there are no relevant regulations from any government.

These traps can be set in a matter of days or hours. They are usually triggered when the demand for an asset exceeds the number of holders willing to sell it. Buyers then increase their bids by attracting more sellers and pushing the market upwards.

Institutional investors are selling their cryptocurrencies in the hope that less skilled market participants will sell theirs, pushing prices down.

When prices fall to the desired level set by those who set the trap, they then buy back large quantities of the asset, pushing prices up and making a profit. The reason institutional investors can do this is, obviously, because when they sell their huge quantities they move the entire market down. Their every action is immediately felt in the markets. That's why there is always a lot of attention paid to what the various accounts holding large amounts of cryptocurrencies are doing.

Wyckoff Investment Method

Now we will learn a method that will help us understand the ups and downs of the market. So, we will be able to predict to a certain extent what is going to happen in the market. It is one of the most famous methods. It is used to some extent by everyone in the stock market and, of course, in cryptocurrencies.

To understand what it does, we only need to observe that cryptocurrency prices are constantly moving up and down due to large and small forces. These forces push the prices up and down constantly. This method helps us understand how to identify these forces and their influence, so that we can learn to predict the movements of cryptocurrency prices. The Wyckoff method is a study of the relationship between supply and demand forces.

It was first developed by Richard D. Wyckoff, a trader and market forecaster, who started his business in 1888 as a 15-year-old stock runner. Wyckoff observed the activities of a group of well-informed, more experienced traders/investors. This group included J.P. Morgan, Andrew Carnegie, James Keene, Jesse Livermore, and many others.

They were the best traders in the stock market. They knew how to analyze the market, why and how it moved, and how to take advantage of the changes. They also had the ability to influence market trends and price direction.

Wyckoff ran his own brokerage firm, so he was in a better position to observe how the best traders carefully planned and executed their trades. Then, Wyckoff incorporated their best practices with his original ideas and created a chart-based method, based on various principles, techniques, and laws, to monitor and trade with market trends in harmony. Soon, Wycoff and his method were loved by Wall Street, and have been used by most traders ever since.

The Wyckoff rules and method

The Wyckoff method reveals the intentions of super traders in the stock market and, in our case, in the cryptocurrency market. The basis of this method is the analysis of trading volume and price.

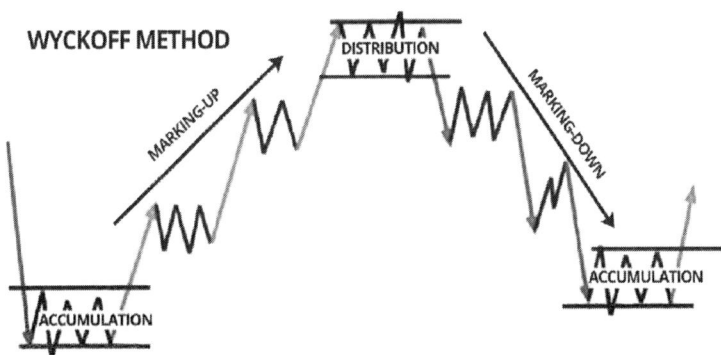

Wyckoff believed that the behavior of big moves and price was indicative of something and was the key to predicting future market movements. These observations led him to believe that the stock market operated according to a set of three laws.

The Law of Cause and Effect

For the price of a stock to change (the result), there must be a cause that caused it. The effect is directly proportional to this cause.

The Law of Supply and Demand

If an item is offered in a very small quantity, the value of that item will increase to create the need for supply to meet demand. Or, when something is offered in excessive quantities, then the value of that item will decrease to attract the demand needed to absorb that supply. The law is about the simple operation of these two factors.

The Law of Effort Versus Result

Effort refers to the trading volume that moves in relation to a stock (in our case, in relation to the cryptocurrency), and result refers to the movement of the price of the stock or cryptocurrency. If there is effort, the result must be proportional to that effort and cannot be separated from it. If it is not, it is an indication that there are other principles at work and what exactly is happening must be found by some other method or with some other data.

The action of the price and the moving volume must be in harmony. If you have a lot of volume, you should see a lot of movement. If you don't see movement, you need to find out what is happening. You need to learn to use your tools to evaluate the result (price action) against the corresponding effort (volume).

Traders apply this data to observe how institutions enter the market and when it is the right time for them to enter.

Understanding the current supply and demand structure of a cryptocurrency allows you to predict future price trends. The rule is very simple: when demand exceeds supply, cryptocurrency prices go up, and when supply is higher than demand, prices fall to create more demand.

Traders should choose cryptocurrencies in relation to the price targets they intend to achieve when trading. Also, don't forget the law of cause and effect, which states that trades should only be made when there is a significant cause that causes an effect. For example, when Tesla bought Bitcoin, it had a large positive effect (result) on the entire market.

The Wyckoff method also sets out some other important steps that traders can use to know whether a cryptocurrency is worth buying or selling. Familiarity with these steps and an understanding of market supply and demand can help you know if using the method during periods of market decline or a market rally is warranted.

Also, knowing when your cryptocurrency prices will rise or fall is beneficial to your money's performance. It is very important for traders, who want to buy when the market is undervalued during a downturn, to be sure that it will reverse in a rally.

So we conclude that cryptocurrency prices change for various reasons. Knowing these reasons is what determines whether you will win or not.

Some people tend to believe that it is impossible to predict changes, let alone just by looking at graphs. However, there are several people who believe that observing graphs and past price movements can help you predict the price of a cryptocurrency and determine when to buy or sell.

The Wyckoff Method is an important tool used by many successful institutional and professional traders. This method can be applied in any time frame, in any free market.

A practical and effective understanding of the method gives you an advantage when trading at the same time as large institutions, pension funds, and investment banks, which start and stop big trends. Finally, it will allow you to learn to determine the overall direction of the market.

The Wyckoff method teaches traders to predict market turns by understanding the 3 laws described above. Along with practice and observation of the market based on these 3 rules, you will be ready to act at the right time.

The Best Ways to Learn Technical Analysis

One thing that anyone new to cryptocurrencies should be aware of is technical analysis. Technical analysis is the study of charts and patterns, but it can also include aspects of risk management and how the economy behaves. The goal of technical analysis is to identify good opportunities and exploit them using a disciplined, rules-based approach that maximizes long-term returns. Let's look at some of the best ways to learn technical analysis, even if you're a beginner, without having to risk money in the market.

Beginning traders should turn to books and online courses to get an in-depth understanding of technical analysis. I will not go into the entire topic here; however, I will mention some basic facts to give a global knowledge on the subject. If one searches, one will find many online trading courses that promise spectacular results, but then fail to deliver the promised results. This is why simulation trading or "paper" trading exists, which can help traders see how technical indicators work in live markets without risking their money.

The first step in learning technical analysis is to gain a fundamental understanding of the basic concepts. You need to learn all the basic concepts around the subject before you can apply the various techniques.

Better education is achieved by reading specialized books, taking online or offline courses, or reading educational websites covering these topics. Many of these can be found for free, but some educational organizations or institutions charge something for extra specialization.

Again, I point out that many online trading courses promise spectacular results, but do not deliver the corresponding results. Novice traders should avoid courses that boast unrealistic returns and seek out instructors who teach the fundamentals of technical analysis.

Many traders develop their own systems and techniques for trading over time. Some are good, some are not so good, and some are cheaters. After all, the companies that offer "secret" trading systems that yield consistent profits probably wouldn't sell them if they were actually profitable (they would keep the secrets to themselves).

Once you have learned the details of technical analysis, the next step is to take the principles you have learned from these lessons and put them into practice through backtesting or "paper" trading.

Backtesting is a term that refers to the testing of a predictive model on historical data. It is a type of testing applied to previous time periods, as well as a special type of validation performed by cross-validation of data. This is a clever way to see if your strategy is working successfully and whether it would have worked successfully in previous periods.

Paper trading is a stock market simulator. It is computer software that reproduces the behavior and characteristics of a stock market, so that users can trade without real financial risk.

Paper trading is also called "virtual stock trading." It is a simulated trading process in which traders can practice investing without committing real money. Through this process one can learn how to play with the data they have learned and which strategy is most efficient, without losing real money, but of course without gaining anything besides experience.

The trader can build an automatic trading strategy. He can use backtesting to see how a set of rules would work using historical data. He could then retest the system to see how it would have performed in recent years.

Of course, we have to keep in mind that trading systems that produce exciting returns using historical data are not guaranteed to perform well in the live market. Also, complex trading systems may appear to perform perfectly using historical data, but they will not be very useful in the future.

Technology is constantly changing. New players are constantly entering the game, so it is not certain that they will continue to have the same pattern forever. The best trading systems use a simple set of rules that make them profitable and are flexible enough to perform well both in the past and in the future. If you have to choose between a simple system with a simple return and a complex one with a very high return, the simple system would of course be the safest.

Traders who trade on their own, without automated trading systems, can work on paper trading to improve their skills. So traders can practice creating trades to see what their performance would be over time. It is a good idea, before putting in any large amount of money, to carefully monitor the performance of these trades to objectively determine how successful your strategies are over time and to practice over a long enough period of time.

There are many companies that give such applications free of charge. Basic training and these apps are free at almost all major companies. Therefore, it is enough to find an app, e.g., Google's, and start working on it until you learn how to earn from trading. There are many platforms that offer simulated trading that resemble live markets, and there is not much difference in quality. So all one needs to do is to find the simplest and easiest platform and start testing it.

Therefore, the best way to learn technical analysis is to gain a solid understanding of the fundamentals, learn a few basic strategies, and apply them using backtesting or paper trading. There is no shortcut to success, but aspiring traders can create a good strategy with the knowledge they have gained, so they have a good sense of how the market works over time. All of this in the end can provide some good profits from trading.

Cryptocurrencies and the S&P 500 Index

A Comparison of Cryptocurrencies with the S&P 500 index

Once upon a time, in the financial markets, the investments that attracted the most attention were commodities, bonds, stocks, and the like. With the rise of cryptocurrencies in recent years, more and more people, especially the younger generation, are starting to replace them with Bitcoin and other cryptocurrencies. But let's compare Bitcoin to the S&P 500 index, one of the most important stock market indices in the United States.

It took a while for the Bitcoin idea to gain popularity. Of course, in that time the reason for its value has changed, and so instead of having value as peer-to-peer electronic cash, Bitcoin is considered by many to be closer to digital gold. However, this innovation quickly emerged and became one of the most valuable asset classes in the world.

Banks and brokers are now offering Bitcoin to their customers, legalizing it as a financial instrument on the same list as commodities, bonds, and stocks. Every day we learn of another bank or institution that has included Bitcoin and other cryptocurrencies in its options.

The S&P 500 or Standard & Poor's 500 is an index that tracks the performance of 500 large companies listed on the United States stock exchange. The index weights companies based on market capitalization, so naturally, the largest companies have a greater influence on the overall performance of the index than smaller companies. The top 5 companies, Apple, Microsoft, Amazon, Tesla, and Alphabet (Google's parent company) alone make up about 23% of the index.

It is considered to be one of the most accurate performance gauges of the companies considered in the index, although some argue that this accuracy has declined as a result of quantitative easing in recent years. However, the majority of market observers closely monitor the S&P 500 as an indicator of the health of markets as a whole or invest in it as a long-term play on U.S. economic growth.

It is obvious that both the cryptocurrency market and the stock market have benefited greatly from monetary policy in recent years. Both markets experienced tremendous growth between 2020 and 2022. Usually, we see both markets affected by similar events, it's just that cryptocurrencies have had large fluctuations. It is very easy to see that cryptocurrencies have double-digit price changes.

There are some who believe that Bitcoin's current price behavior mimics the S&P 500 between 1999 and 2015, albeit at a faster pace. Also, although we are mainly talking about Bitcoin, the same is true for all cryptocurrencies, since Bitcoin's performance can be seen as an overall indicator of cryptocurrencies, because essentially all altcoins follow Bitcoin's behavior.

An important difference also lies in the nature of the asset. The S&P 500 is a basket of 500 long-term companies that have stood the test of time. These companies generate revenue and create real value. Therefore, the intrinsic value of the S&P 500 is quite easily measured using various revenue, cash flow, or earnings models.

As for Bitcoin, its value is much more speculative. You can't really say that there is any product behind it other than that it is intended to be used as electronic money. But that's not true either, since almost no one uses Bitcoin simply as money. They use it like it's a work of art that everyone knows will increase in value because it's rare and in demand. Many other cryptocurrencies, however, have big projects behind them and are also slowly proving their worth over time.

Especially after the first half of 2022, when many projects collapsed, other projects, like Binance, found the opportunity to achieve even more.

Although both the S&P 500 and Bitcoin are valued by the market (through supply and demand), there are no revenue streams, dividend payments, or annual reports to measure the potential value of Bitcoin. This lack of data is part of the reason why Bitcoin is much closer to a commodity than a stock market index. Discussing the differences and similarities between Bitcoin, S&P 500, Real Estate, Gold, and other financial instruments is very interesting, it's fun, you can argue with a lot of people, but ultimately it can be a bit counterproductive. We can debate endlessly about the superiority of one over the other or just find their differences and point them out. All asset classes have their uses, and diversification can go a long way to making a portfolio more profitable.

In my opinion, one should be able to have a global knowledge of all this and study enough to understand what it is that makes markets move. There are many things that can affect the economy at any given time, and no one can guarantee that gold, stocks, or cryptocurrencies will be the most valuable tomorrow. It's good to be in all of them to a degree, but it may be best to focus more on one that you prefer for personal reasons.

As you study other markets, you may find an advantage you've been ignoring or realize that the unexplored market is much more interesting than you thought. The point is to try new things and judge based on that experience and the study you are doing at the time, not on assumptions. I think experimenting with each market will help you learn what is most worthwhile to you. Considering the correlation between markets, this understanding is extremely beneficial to gain more profits in the future.

In conclusion, there is a use for both the S&P 500 and Bitcoin. But personally, I think Bitcoin is superior to the S&P 500 because money in the future will be electronic and all of the S&P 500 companies will eventually need Bitcoin, but Bitcoin will not need any of those companies. I suggest experimenting with different financial instruments and broadening your horizons. You may struggle for a while, but in the end, you will gain new skills and knowledge.

Do your research, try new things, and let's keep making money!

Mistakes We Make in Investing

When we talk about investment we are always dealing with information, and the most common problem in investment is misinformation. A simple piece of misinformation can cause the entire market to fall and cause people to start selling low. For this reason, when we hear a piece of information, we need to check which platform we are getting our data and information from.

I have found some good platforms for information on cryptocurrencies. They are *Decrypt.com, Coindesk.com, Cointelegraph.com, Cnbc.com, Marketwatch.com, Newsbtc.com, Bitcoin.com, Finance.yahoo.com, Investing.com,* and, of course, in Greek, my website *Cryptonea.gr*.

Here I should stress that if one does not want to become a long-term investor, one should learn trading. Trading has a different philosophy and does not work so much with the rules of investing as with the rules one learns in trading, as well as the odd market manipulations.

Michael Saylor, who, he says, invested in Facebook before it went public and in Apple before music was even on its phones, also says that if you want to give knowledge to 5 billion people, then you have to have it in electronic form. With the same logic, if you want to give wealth to 5 billion people, then you have to give it in electronic form, and what better way than through Bitcoin.

When asked if he was worried about the price of Bitcoin at a time when it had fallen quite a bit, he said he was not a trader but a long-term investor. He also said, "If I was a trader I would be constantly stressed and would be looking at articles, etc. all the time. But I believe in technology, and I think digital has a future."

In light of this statement, I can say that being a long-term cryptocurrency investor is a decision that makes you sleep easy. It is the future not because I believe it, but because someone who has achieved a lot in this industry believes it. And there's the other thing about investing, which is to follow some successful people in the industry and do things they say, which make sense. Everyone should find 2 or 3 such people and follow them faithfully until they succeed themselves.

<u>The mistake we can make is to not listen to those who have succeeded in this area and instead listen to information here and there that seems to influence the price at the time. This practice is what will cause us to lose money and act weakly in times when we need to be steady in our investments.</u>

Another big mistake is that people get "hooked" on negative articles because these articles get too much attention. This causes them to lose confidence in the project they invested in in the first place and they usually lose it at a time when the market is down. It is important to choose the project based on its value and the services it provides. So, no matter what happens, the investor will not lose confidence and will not sell at a bad time out of anxiety or fear that the project they have chosen will not succeed.

The Number One Secret of My Success

Now, I'll tell you my number one secret of success that worked well for me and changed my entire life forever! It's one thing that I implemented completely by accident and it worked positively for me because I did it to help the people. It completely changed my life, increasing my income 20 times, increasing my personal connections and helping me achieve all my goals.

That one thing was that I started giving without asking for anything in return. It's something anyone can do in any field and it will help them succeed. But what does that mean in practice?

We have heard the phrase "if you give to the universe, the universe will give back to you." As salespeople, we are always mindful of what our customers will get from us, if and when they give it to us first… You see, somehow, we end up going back to taking first before giving, when we should have given something first.

I was operating incorrectly for several years. I thought I was giving first and then receiving, but eventually I saw that I was asking first and then giving. I would ask for the money or whatever first and then give the information or service. Even though my payment could practically arrive after the service was delivered to the client, I had actually asked for my return from the beginning and hadn't given anything free or extra before asking for what I wanted.

This generated some income, but it never got me where I wanted to go. At some point when I started to make the change, out of intuition and without realizing or thinking about it, I realized that when you are rising yourself, things are much simpler and easier compared to the times when you are down or at the bottom.

The change was to start giving in abundance and not asking. I created my YouTube channel and started giving information to people generously. I loved giving and then helping all these people succeed, and that was the key to being successful in everything.

The more I kept giving, the more people followed me on my YouTube channel and that's how the sponsorships started coming in. People who were watching me and gaining something from what they were learning wanted to give me something in return. For example, once I went to buy a small item and the owner of the store gave me a gift of a cologne because he was watching me every day on his computer. This even happened in the early days when I had a small audience.

That doesn't mean I didn't have to discipline myself, improve, study, change my way of communicating, and put in long hours of work for my self-improvement. I had to do all of that. But at the same time, I was also putting in hard work. At the end of the day, especially for the first period, I had to generate extra income from something else because expenses were running up and that caused extra stress. But the bottom line is that I changed the way I operated, first giving and then asking, whereas before I was asking and then giving.

Whether you're an employee, a business person, an actor, or anything else, you need to see how you can start giving. And I see it right now, just by giving I have so much influx that I don't have time to manage it. People around me are now so willing to give that I don't even have to try to sell something as a salesman or insist until someone buys my product. This is a big change from how I was before, where I had to talk to people every day to sell a service and, even after all that work, many times I didn't succeed or get it done to the level I wanted.

So, my advice is for everyone out there to find something they can give generously and give it. People are looking for solutions to survive. If someone gives them something that helps them and solves their problem, then they will gain their attention and trust. Once one gets these, then the money is already in their wallet.

So that's my advice and the number one secret to my success. I wish I had realized this years ago, because I could always give so much, but I was stuck asking first, when instead I should have given first.

20 Top Crypto Projects

The following Crypto projects that I present are some of the best available on the market at the time of writing. In the future they may be different. Presenting these projects is not an encouragement to invest in them in any way! The recommended projects are now widely accepted as top projects with potential.

However, proper study and understanding is required before choosing to invest in any of these projects. One needs to monitor their progress because nothing stays the same forever and there is no promise or guarantee of future success or performance!

There are certainly other very good projects on the market, perhaps with better prospects. But, at the time of writing, these are some of the top projects worth looking at.

Bitcoin (BTC)

It goes without saying that the number 1 position could not belong to any other project than Bitcoin. We have said a lot about this project and we can say a lot more.

It is the first official cryptocurrency. There will be only 21 million coins in circulation, making it rarer than even gold. If a Bitcoin is lost, there is no known way to get it back into circulation, which makes it even more valuable!

The whole history of Bitcoin is wonderful. Although years have passed, and the price has gone up too much, so that it no longer seems that one can make much profit with small investments, this currency is still the strongest one and the one that has made the most progress.

In fact, I believe, like many other cryptocurrency experts, that Bitcoin still has a lot to offer. It doesn't seem hard to me to reach $1 million in value within the next few years. In fact, I think it's a sure thing. But does anyone have the guts to invest now and wait another 5 or 7 or even 10 years without bending on the bad days and without sweetening the good ones? Can he hold on so that he doesn't go for a short and nice profit, and expect to see himself at the top after many years?

That's the challenge we have to go through with Bitcoin, because it's sure to go up, and it's going to go up a lot.

There are 21 million Bitcoins (less to be exact) and there are still no regulations in almost all countries that allow large organizations and institutions to enter and invest in Bitcoin legally and easily, while they can invest in gold or in a company like Meta. Imagine what will happen when in America and Europe organizations will be able to invest in Bitcoin legally and easily! In my opinion, the value of Bitcoin will reach over $1 million at that point and will continue to rise no matter what happens.

No matter how many better projects they come up with, Bitcoin is now like a work of art. People don't care anymore what they can do with it, they just care about having 1 Bitcoin and that's enough.

Based on this and much more, I believe that Bitcoin will forever remain the number one cryptocurrency, and its value will continue to rise. Sure, it will go through some ups and downs, but in the long run it will continue to rise.

Ethereum (ETH)

Similarly with Bitcoin, I couldn't help but have Ether in the number 2 position. It is the second most powerful cryptocurrency in the world, and many other projects are working on its blockchain. It has better practical functionality than Bitcoin, and that makes it the second most powerful cryptocurrency. Also, much of the NFT market is on its network, and the team behind the project is constantly working on improving it.

It is the second favorite project for major investors in the world. This is mainly because it inspires great confidence in people entering the world of cryptocurrencies.

What is Ethereum (ETH)?

Ethereum is a decentralized, open-source blockchain system that has its own cryptocurrency, Ether. ETH acts as a platform for many other cryptocurrencies, as well as for running decentralized smart contracts.

Ethereum was first described in 2013 by Vitalik Buterin. Buterin, along with other co-founders, secured funding for the project in an online participatory sale in the summer of 2014, and officially launched the blockchain on July 30, 2015.

The goal of Ethereum is to become a global platform for decentralized applications, allowing users from around the world to write and run software without worrying about censorship, downtime, and fraud.

What makes Ethereum unique?

Ethereum's key innovation was to design a platform that allows it to run smart contracts using the blockchain, which further enhances the already existing benefits of smart contract technology. Ethereum's blockchain was designed, according to co-founder Gavin Wood, as a kind of "computer for the whole planet," theoretically capable of making any program more censorship-resistant and less prone to fraud by running it on a global network of distributed public nodes.

How many Ethereum (ETH) coins are in circulation?

In August 2020, there were approximately 112 million ETH coins in circulation, 72 million of which were issued on the genesis block – the first block on the Ethereum blockchain. Of that, 60 million was allocated to the original 2014 equity investors who funded the project and 12 million was given to the development fund.

The remaining amount has been issued in the form of block rewards to miners on the Ethereum network. The initial reward in 2015 was 5 ETH per block, which was later reduced to 3 ETH in late 2017, and then to 2 ETH in early 2019.

One of the most important differences between Bitcoin and Ethereum is that in the latter, the total supply is not limited. Ethereum developers justify this by saying that they don't want to have a "fixed security budget" for the network. The ability to adjust the ETH issuance rate via consensus allows the network to maintain the minimum required issuance with sufficient security.

Solana (SOL)

Solana is a highly functional open-source project. Banks rely on the nature of blockchain technology, which has the advantage of being provided with a free license, to provide decentralized finance (DeFi) solutions. While the concept and initial work on the project began in 2017, Solana was officially launched in March 2020 by the Solana Foundation based in Geneva, Switzerland.

The Solana protocol is designed to facilitate the creation of decentralized applications (DApps). It aims to improve scalability by introducing a Proof of History (PoH) algorithm in conjunction with the blockchain's underlying Proof of Stake consensus. Proof of History is an algorithm that provides proof that something happened before or after a known event, rather than relying on a timestamp.

Due to its innovative hybrid consensual model, Solana enjoys interest from both micro-traders and institutional traders. A major focus for the Solana Foundation is to make decentralized finance more accessible on a larger scale.

Anatoly Yakovenko is the most important person behind Solana. His professional career started at Qualcomm (American multinational telecommunications products and services company), where he quickly rose through the ranks to become Senior Staff Engineer Manager in 2015. Later, his career path changed and Yakovenko took a new position as a software engineer at Dropbox.

In 2017, Yakovenko started working on a project that would later be implemented as Solana. He teamed up with his colleague at Qualcomm, Greg Fitzgerald, and they founded a project called Solana Labs. Attracting several other former Qualcomm colleagues in the process, the Solana protocol and SOL token were released in 2020.

One of the key innovations that Solana brings to the table is the Proof of History developed by Anatoly Yakovenko. This concept allows for greater scalability of the protocol, which in turn enhances usability.

Solana is well known in the cryptocurrency space because of the incredibly short processing times offered by the blockchain. Solana's hybrid protocol enables significantly reduced validation times for both transaction execution and smart contracts. With lightning-fast processing times, Solana has also attracted considerable institutional interest.

The Solana protocol is intended to serve both individual users and corporate clients. One of Solana's main promises to customers is that they will not be surprised by increased charges and fees. The protocol is designed in such a way that it has low transaction costs, while guaranteeing scalability and fast processing.

Solana has been in the Top 10 for quite some time. This came after an impressive run where Solana's price gained over 700% since mid-July 2021. The release of the Degenerate Ape NFT collection drove the SOL price to an all-time high of over $60. Since then, it has grown largely due to more developer activity in the Solana ecosystem, higher institutional interest, the growing DeFi ecosystem, as well as the rise of NFTs and the gaming industry in Solana. Solana's price has now dropped quite a bit from the highest level it reached, but is still many times higher than when it started.

Solana has received much praise for its speed and performance, and has even been described as a rival that can be compared to Ethereum and challenge the dominant smart contracts platform. However, the network has been plagued by repeated outages that have undermined its value and ambitions to become the "Visa of crypto." In addition, its ecosystem has been accused of favoring venture capitalists with unfair proof.

The Solana Foundation announced that a total of 489 million SOL will be in circulation. The distribution of SOL token is as follows: 16.23% went to an initial sale, 12.92% was given to a foundation sale, 12.79% was distributed among the group members, and 10.46% was given to the Solana Foundation. The remaining tokens have already been released for public and private sales, or will be released to the market at a later date.

The price of Solana at the time of the initial sale, which took place on April 5, 2018, was $0.04. The recent All Time High in price represents an impressive Return on Investment (ROI) of 5400 times.

XRP Ledger (XRPL)

The XRP Ledger (XRPL) was established in 2012 by David Schwartz, Jed McCaleb, and Arthur Britto, with the native currency XRP. Their vision was to create a faster and more energy-efficient alternative to the Bitcoin blockchain. The company, now known as Ripple, was founded in the same year by these individuals along with Chris Larsen.

The XRPL, introduced in 2021, stands as an open-source, permissionless, and decentralized technology, offering a range of distinct advantages. Notably, it boasts low transaction costs, with fees as minimal as $0.0002, ensuring cost-effective transactions. Its efficiency shines through in the speed department, with the capability to settle transactions in just 3 to 5 seconds. XRPL is also highly scalable, handling up to 1,500 transactions per second. Moreover, it prides itself on being environmentally conscious, touting a carbon-neutral and energy-efficient profile.

One standout feature of XRPL is its incorporation of a decentralized exchange (DEX) and built-in tokenization capabilities within its protocol. Since its launch in 2012, XRPL has consistently closed 70 million ledgers, showcasing its robust and reliable operation.

Versatility and Utility:

XRPL is not confined to a single use case. It offers a wide range of applications, from micropayments and DeFi to upcoming support for NFTs. Developers have access to robust tools and resources, with support for Python, Java, and JavaScript. The XRPL website hosts tutorials to help developers get started with different coding languages, app development, account management, and more.

Beyond the native XRP coin, XRPL serves as the foundation for solutions that address inefficiencies in fields like remittance and asset tokenization. The five main applications currently dominating XRPL are payments, tokenization, DeFi, central bank digital currencies (CBDCs), and stablecoins.

80 billion XRP tokens were gifted to Ripple by the architects of XRPL. These tokens were intended to fuel the development of use cases, including the global payments network known as RippleNet.

XRPL takes a unique approach to transaction validation using a Federated Consensus mechanism. Transactions are confirmed through a consensus protocol, where independent servers, referred to as validators, reach an agreement on transaction order and outcomes. Every server processes transactions consistently, and as long as a transaction adheres to the protocol, it is confirmed instantly. Transparency is key, and anyone can operate a validator. Currently, there are over 150 validators worldwide, operated by universities, businesses, and individuals. This mechanism ensures that verified transactions can proceed without a single point of failure, as no single participant makes independent decisions.

Ripple and the SEC:

Ripple Labs, the creators of XRP, has been embroiled in a legal battle with the U.S. Securities and Exchange Commission (SEC) since late 2020. The core issue revolves around whether XRP qualifies as a security.

The SEC initiated a lawsuit on December 22, 2020, alleging that Ripple Labs and two of its executives conducted a $1.3 billion unregistered security sale in XRP. The lawsuit has sparked intense debates, with Ripple vehemently disputing the claims and asserting SEC bias.

The SEC employs the "Howey test" to determine whether a cryptocurrency is a security, and it hinges on whether an asset is sold with the expectation of profits from the efforts of others. While most similar cases resulted in settlements, Ripple opted to contest the SEC's allegations and secured a significant victory when a federal judge rejected the SEC's bid to appeal their loss in October 2023, marking a notable milestone for the entire crypto industry.

Polygon (MATIC)

Polygon (formerly Matic Network) is the first, well-structured, easy-to-use platform for scaling and deploying Ethereum infrastructure. Its core component is the Polygon SDK, a modular, flexible framework that supports the creation of multiple types of applications.

Polygon effectively converts Ethereum into a complete multi-chain system (also known as the Internet of Blockchains). This multi-chain system is similar to others such as Polkadot, Cosmos, Avalanche, etc. with the advantages of security, live ecosystem, and open accessibility of Ethereum.

MATIC will continue to exist and play an increasingly important role, safeguarding the system and enabling governance.

Polygon is a level 2 scaling solution supported by Binance and Coinbase. The project seeks to boost mass cryptocurrency adoption by solving scalability issues across multiple blockchains.

Polygon combines the Plasma Framework and the Proof of Stake blockchain architecture. The Plasma Framework, used by Polygon as proposed by Ethereum co-founder Vitalik Buterin, allows for easy execution of scalable and autonomous smart contracts.

Polygon boasts up to 65,000 transactions per second on a single sidechain (a secondary blockchain connected to the main blockchain with a two-way link). It has a respectable block confirmation time that is less than two seconds. The Plasma Framework also enables the creation of globally available decentralized financial applications on a single core blockchain.

The Plasma Framework allows Polygon to host an unlimited number of decentralized applications on its infrastructure, without facing the usual drawbacks common to the Proof of Work blockchain. So far, Polygon has attracted more than 50 DApps on the Ethereum sidechain with Proof of Stake security.

MATIC, Polygon's native token, is an ERC-20 token running on the Ethereum blockchain. The tokens are used for payment services on Polygon and as a settlement currency between users operating within the Polygon ecosystem. Transaction fees on Polygon sidechains are also paid in MATIC.

Who are the founders of Polygon?

Polygon was released in October 2017. It was founded by Jaynti Kanani, Sandeep Nailwal, and Anurag Arjun, along with two experienced blockchain developers and a business consultant.

Before moving to its network in 2019, the Polygon team contributed a lot to the Ethereum ecosystem. The team worked on implementing the Plasma MVP, the WalletConnect protocol, and the widely used Dagger event notification engine on Ethereum.

Co-founder Jaynti Kanani, a software developer, web application developer, and blockchain engineer, currently serves as Polygon's CEO.

Jaynti Kanani played an integral role in the implementation of the Web3, Plasma, and WalletConnect protocol on Ethereum. Prior to his involvement with blockchain, he worked as a data scientist at *Housing.com*.

The co-founder and COO (Chief Operating Officer) of Polygon, Sandeep Nailwal is a blockchain developer and entrepreneur. Prior to co-founding

Polygon, he was the CEO of Scopeweaver and CTO (Chief Technical Officer) of Welspun Group.

Anurag Arjun is the only non-developer co-founder of Polygon. As a product manager, he was at IRIS Business, SNL Financial, Dexter Consultancy, and Cognizant Technologies.

What makes Polygon unique?

Polygon calls itself a level 2 scaling solution, which means the project is not looking to upgrade the current base level blockchain any time soon. The project is focused on reducing the complexity of scalability and instantaneous blockchain transactions.

Polygon uses a custom version of the Plasma Framework built on Proof of Stake checkpoints on the Ethereum main chain. This unique technology allows each sidechain in Polygon to achieve up to 65,536 transactions per block.

Commercially, Polygon's sidechains are designed to support a variety of decentralized finance (DeFi) protocols available in the Ethereum ecosystem.

While Polygon currently only supports the Ethereum core chain, the network plans to expand support for additional core chains based on community suggestions and consensus. This would make Polygon an interoperable, decentralized level 2 blockchain platform.

How many Polygon coins (MATIC) are in circulation?

MATIC tokens are released on a monthly basis. There are currently 4,877,830,774 MATIC in circulation and the maximum supply is 10,000,000,000 MATIC.

In the initial private sale in 2017, 3.8% of the maximum MATIC offering was issued. In the launchpad sale in April 2019, 19% of the total offer was sold. The MATIC price was $0.00263 per token and raised $5 million.

The remaining MATIC tokens are distributed as follows:

Group Tokens: 16% of the total offer.

Consultant Tokens: 4% of the total offer.

Network Operations Tokens: 12% of the total offer.

Foundation Tokens: 21.86% of the total offer.

Ecosystem Tokens: 23.33% of the total offer.

According to the release schedule, all tokens will be released by December 2022.

Where can you buy Polygon (MATIC)?

Being one of the projects that contributed greatly to the development of the Ethereum ecosystem, MATIC is popular among online exchanges that focus on DeFi. The top exchanges where you can buy, sell, and trade MATIC right now are Binance, Coinbase Pro, Huobi Global, and KuCoin.

Cardano (ADA)

Cardano is a blockchain Proof of Stake platform. It says its goal is to enable "pioneers, innovators, and visionaries" to change the world for the better.

Cardano was founded by Charles Hoskinson, who was also one of the co-founders of the Ethereum network. He is the CEO of IOHK, the company that created the Cardano blockchain.

In an interview for CoinMarketCap's Crypto Titans series, Hoskinson said he got involved with cryptocurrencies in 2011 – with mining and trading. He explained that his first professional involvement with the industry was in 2013, when he created a Bitcoin seminar that was eventually attended by more than 80,000 students.

In addition to being a technology entrepreneur, Hoskinson is also a mathematician. In 2020, his company donated $500,000 worth of ADA to the University of Wyoming's blockchain research and development lab.

It is an open-source project and aims to "redistribute power from large institutions to individuals," helping to create a safer society that is transparent and fair.

Cardano was founded in 2017. The ADA token is designed to ensure that its holders can participate in the operation of the network. Thanks to this, those who hold the cryptocurrency have the right to vote on any proposed changes to the software.

The team behind the project says it aims to enable the development of decentralized applications and smart contracts, and has achieved this to a good extent.

Cardano is used by agricultural companies to track fresh products from the field to the consumer's plate. Other products created on the platform allow their certificates to be stored in a tamper-proof manner and allow retailers to combat the movement of counterfeit products.

The project ensures that all technology developed goes through a peer review process, meaning that bold ideas can be challenged before they are validated. According to Cardano's team, this academic rigor helps the blockchain to be resilient and stable, increasing the chances of being prepared for potential pitfalls in advance.

In 2020, Cardano carried out the Shelley upgrade, which aimed to make its blockchain "50 to 100 times more decentralized" than other major blockchains. At the time, Hoskinson predicted that this would pave the way for hundreds of assets to circulate on his network.

There is a maximum offer of 45 billion ADA. In total, approximately 16% of the total ADA offering was allocated to the founders of the project, while the remaining 84% was allocated to investors.

Flux (FLUX)

Flux is the new generation of scalable decentralized cloud infrastructure. You can simply deploy, manage and build your applications on multiple servers simultaneously. It's ready for Web 3.0, DApps, and more.

The Flux Ecosystem is a fully functional suite of decentralized computing services and blockchain-as-a-service solutions, offering a cross-functional, decentralized development environment that resembles AWS (Amazon Web

Services – an Amazon subsidiary that provides cloud computing platforms and connections to other applications).

The Flux Ecosystem consists of the following components, all of which are fully developed and functional.

Flux is a native GPU (Graphics Processing Unit) currency with the ability to mine Proof of Work.

It has a next-generation decentralized Web3 computing network with more than 2600+ Flux nodes, located all over the world and growing (at the time of writing), with a lot of computing power. They provide about 12,850+ vCore CPUs, 40+ terabytes of RAM, and 975+ terabytes of storage. Anyone can support a Flux node anywhere in the world if they provide the required security and Flux hardware for one of the three levels of Flux nodes.

Flux nodes can be run on Raspberry Pi/Home PCs/Servers/VPS hardware from anywhere in the world.

Flux node operators are rewarded with Flux through block rewards, but they are also able to earn other cryptocurrencies by hosting specific DApps on their nodes.

FluxOS is an operating system that runs on top of the Linux operating system. It manages the network by verifying and benchmarking computing power, deploying, running, and load balancing decentralized applications, managing XDAO governance, and more. The network currently hosts more than 30 DApps, including blockchain infrastructure, social media, data predictions, web pages, games, and file storage.

Parallel chain interoperability. It is a DeFi bridge that provides access to large decentralized centers. It provides cross-functionality with other blockchains and access to DeFi.

Zelcore is the official Flux wallet. It is a wallet where you can hold many different assets. It has the ability to integrate large centralized and decentralized exchanges. It works on computers and mobile devices.

Flux is an open source, community-driven project. It is independent, with no external investors. As such, Flux is distributed fairly with no coins mined in advance or distributions for anyone other than holders, miners, and node operators. The project is highly committed to building a true decentralized future, remaining independent, and constantly pushing for innovation in blockchain technology.

The Flux economic model highly incentivizes holders, GPU miners, and node operators through airdrops (certain amounts of a cryptocurrency given for free to encourage its use and popularity), mining, and node rewards. Node operators can also earn additional cryptocurrencies through partnerships and paid app hosting.

The last reason is the one that I believe will make Flux even more successful, as it will bring a lot of audience to the network when Ethereum works with Proof of Stake and miners are looking for their next big project.

Cosmos (ATOM)

Another big project is Cosmos. The co-founders of Tendermint – the gateway to the Cosmos ecosystem – were Jae Kwon, Zarko Milosevic, and Ethan Buchman. Although Kwon is still listed as the main architect, he stepped down as CEO in 2020. He claims he is still involved in the project, but is primarily focused on other initiatives. He has been replaced as CEO of Tendermint by Peng Zhong, and the entire board has been refreshed quite a bit. Their goals include improving the experience for developers, creating an enthusiastic community for Cosmos, and creating educational resources so more people know what this network can do.

In short, Cosmos is self-funded as a project that solves some of the difficult problems facing the blockchain industry. It aims to provide an antidote to "slow, expensive, unscalable, and environmentally harmful" Proof of Work protocols, such as those used by Bitcoin, by offering an ecosystem of connected blockchains.

Another goal of the project is to make blockchain technology less complicated and difficult for developers, thanks to a modular framework that demystifies decentralized applications. Last but not least, an Inter-Blockchain Communication protocol makes it easier for blockchain networks to communicate with each other, thus preventing fragmentation in the industry.

The origins of Cosmos date back to 2014, when Tendermint, a key partner of the network, was founded. In 2016, a white paper on Cosmos was published, and a token sale was held the following year. ATOM tokens are earned through a hybrid Proof of Stake algorithm and help maintain the security of the Cosmos Hub, the project's flagship blockchain. This cryptocurrency also plays a role in network governance.

A major concern for some nodes in the cryptocurrency industry centers on the levels of fragmentation seen in blockchain networks. There are hundreds of them, but very few of them can communicate with each other. Cosmos aims to turn this around by making it possible.

Cosmos is described as "Blockchain 3.0." As I mentioned earlier, a big goal is to ensure that its infrastructure is simple to use. To this end, the Cosmos software development kit focuses on modular blockchain. A module is a piece of code that can be linked to other pieces of code so that they all perform a specific task together. This makes it easy to build a network using pieces of code that already exist. In the long run, they hope that this will result in easier development of complex applications.

Scalability is another priority. This means that more transactions can be processed in a second than on most old-fashioned blockchains, like Bitcoin and Ethereum. For blockchains to fully succeed, they will need to be able to keep up with demand, dominate existing payment processors or websites, and become even better.

ATOM has a very specific total amount of coins, which is 260,906,513 coins, to be exact. It's worth noting that not all of these cryptocurrencies are currently available, but they are also not mined – instead, they are earned through staking.

Two private sales took place in January 2017, followed by a public sale in April of the same year. Analyzing the token distribution, approximately 80% was distributed to investors, while the remaining 20% was split between the two companies All In Bits and Interchain Foundation.

Arbitrum (ARB)

Arbitrum, introduced as an Ethereum layer-two (L2) scaling solution, aspires to address some of Ethereum's core limitations. It harnesses optimistic rollups to enhance speed, scalability, and cost-efficiency while retaining the security and compatibility of Ethereum. Notably, it achieves higher throughput and lower fees compared to Ethereum by relocating a significant portion of computation and storage off-chain.

Central to Arbitrum's governance is its native token, ARB. The development team, Offchain Labs, has transitioned towards a decentralized autonomous organization (DAO) structure known as the Arbitrum DAO. ARB holders wield voting power over critical decisions, including protocol upgrades, feature development, fund allocation, and the election of a Security Council.

Looking ahead to 2023, Arbitrum has set an ambitious roadmap. It includes the launch of Orbit, a layer-three solution, enabling developers to deploy programs in widely-used languages like Rust and C++. Furthermore, they aim to expand their validator set to include more independent institutional validators and migrate their protocol to layer two with Arbitrum One.

A notable milestone occurred on March 16, 2023, with Arbitrum's highly anticipated ARB token airdrop. Early users and DAOs actively participating on Arbitrum were rewarded with 12.75% of the total supply through a point-based system, based on their interactions with the network until the cutoff date of March 1, 2023. The token generation event is slated for March 23, 2023.

The Minds Behind Arbitrum:

Offchain Labs, a New York-based development company, is the driving force behind Arbitrum. Its founders, Ed Felten, Steven Goldfeder, and Harry

Kalodner, bring their wealth of experience in computer science, cryptography, and blockchain to the project. Notably, Ed Felten is a computer science professor at Princeton and has served as President Obama's Deputy CTO. He holds the role of Chief Scientist at Offchain Labs. Steven Goldfeder, a computer scientist and entrepreneur with a Ph.D. from Princeton, serves as the CEO, while Harry Kalodner, a computer scientist and Ph.D. candidate at Princeton, takes on the role of CTO.

In 2021, Offchain Labs secured $120 million in a Series B funding round, led by Lightspeed Venture Partners and valued at $1.2 billion. Notable investors include Polychain Capital, Pantera Capital, and Mark Cuban, among others.

Arbitrum distinguishes itself with its use of optimistic rollups. It offers several advantages over other optimistic rollup solutions, such as:

Compatibility: Arbitrum supports unmodified EVM contracts and transactions, allowing Ethereum DApps to run on Arbitrum without code changes.

Scalability: With a capacity for thousands of transactions per second, Arbitrum maintains low fees, fast finality, and Ethereum's security.

Flexibility: Developers can deploy programs in popular languages like Rust and C++ using Stylus, an upcoming EVM+ equivalence feature.

Decentralization: Arbitrum's network relies on a decentralized network of validators, eliminating the need for a centralized operator or sequencer to order transactions. Validators secure the network by staking ARB tokens and earn fees for their efforts.

Arbitrum boasts a thriving ecosystem of DApps, wallets, tools, and partners, positioning it as a leading Ethereum scaling solution. Notable protocols available on the network include GMX, Treasure, Camelot, Radiant Capital, Vela Exchange, ZyberSwap, Dopex, PlutusDAO, TridentDAO, Jones DAO, and more.

This robust ecosystem reflects in the Total Value Locked (TVL) metric, which peaked at $3.2 billion in November 2021 and currently stands at around $1.85 billion.

ARB Token Overview:

The ARB token is the native governance token of Arbitrum, and it was launched on March 23, 2023. ARB holders have a pivotal role in governing the Arbitrum network by participating in governance proposals for Arbitrum One and Arbitrum Nova chains, influencing DAO treasury funds' utilization. Unlike Ethereum, ARB holders do not pay fees in ARB, but in ETH or other supported ERC-20 tokens.

The total supply of ARB tokens is capped at 10 billion, distributed as follows: 42.78% to the Arbitrum DAO treasury, 26.94% to Offchain Labs teams and advisors, 17.53% to investors, 11.62% as an airdrop to users, and 1.13% as an airdrop to DAOs.

Elrond (EGLD)

Elrond is a blockchain protocol that seeks to offer extremely fast transaction speeds using sharding. The project describes itself as a technology ecosystem for the new internet, which includes Financial Technology (Fintech), decentralized finance, and the Internet of Things (IoT). Its smart contract execution platform is reportedly capable of 15,000 transactions per second, six-second latency, and a transaction cost of $0.001.

The blockchain has a native token known as eGold, or EGLD, which is used to pay network fees, staking, and rewards for validators.

Elrond was first announced in August 2019 and its mainnet was released in July 2020.

Who are the founders of Elrond?

Elrond was founded in late 2017 by brothers Beniamin and Lucian Mincu along with Lucian Todea as a solution to the blockchain scalability problem, which they felt was the most pressing problem the industry was facing.

Prior to Elrond, Beniamin and Lucian Mincu founded MetaChain Capital, a digital asset investment fund, with Beniamin Mincu serving as CEO and Lucian Mincu as Chief Technology Officer. The two also founded ICO Market Data, an aggregator of information about initial coin offerings.

Beniamin Mincu was also responsible for product, marketing, and community for the NEM blockchain platform from 2014 to 2015. He was also an early investor in projects such as Zilliqa (ZIL), Tezos (XTZ), Brave, and Binance. Lucian Mincu has additional experience as a computer engineer and security expert, having worked with Uhrenwerk 24, Cetto, and Liebl Systems.

Todea is a technology entrepreneur who founded and served as CEO of Soft32, a software review and download site, and a partner of mobilPay, a mobile payment app. He is also an angel investor, having invested in biometric technology company TypingDNA and accounting platform SmartBill.

What makes Elrond unique?

Elrond describes itself as a blockchain platform for the new internet economy, decentralized applications, and enterprise use. Its main selling point is its high scalability, stating that it is the first blockchain network to which state, network, and transaction sharding have been implemented. According to its financial document, it seeks to build its ecosystem and establish EGLD as a stored value asset.

To achieve this goal, the network runs on 2,169 validation nodes divided into four pieces, called "shards": three execution shards, each capable of 5,400 transactions per second, and one coordination shard, the "Metachain." Elrond's adaptive state-sharding architecture fully fragments state, transactions, and the network. It can be scaled by adding an additional shard when the processing demand is not met. It was tested to run 263,000 TPS (Transactions Per Second) in a public environment with 1,500 nodes from 29 countries, grouped into 50 shards.

In order to increase adoption, the project also supports developers building on the platform, allowing them to earn 30% of smart contract fees as royalties.

The company retains an EGLD commission for network share performance in its first year of operation, with validation nodes receiving an annual rate of 36%.

How many Elrond (EGLD) coins are in circulation?

The Elrond economic model has a limited supply starting at 20,000,000 EGLD, with new tokens mined to reward network validators. The maximum supply can never exceed 31,415,926 EGLD, but that number will decrease as more transactions are processed.

Elrond's native token was initially made available for purchase through a private sale, in which 19% of its initial offering was sold, with 7.5% being made available immediately after token creation and another 15.41% being released every three months. Elrond also had an initial exchange offer on Binance, where 25% was allocated and sold immediately.

Of the remaining 56%, 7% was set aside for ecosystem rewards, with 50% released immediately and 50% after six months. 8.5% was allocated for marketing, grants, and an accelerator group for DApp developers, with 81.17% released immediately and 9.41% every six months. 2% was allocated to the community fund, with 33.3% released immediately, 33.3% released after six months, and 33.3% released after 12 months. 2.5% was allocated to consultants and released after one year. 19% was allocated for Elrond's founders and core team members, with 10% released after six months, 10% released after 12 months, 15% released after 18, 24, 30, and 36 months, and 20% released after 42 months. Finally, 17% was set aside for the company to support the ecosystem, with 33.3% released immediately for staking only during the first year, and 66.6% in three equal installments over three years, starting after one year.

Elrond's tokens were first issued on the Binance Chain under the name ERD with a total supply of 20 billion tokens. 500 million tokens were burned in November 2019 and minted on the Ethereum blockchain as ERC-20 tokens. The company launched a token exchange event in September 2020 for token holders, where they could exchange ERC-20 and BEP-2 tokens for mainnet EGLD tokens. During the process, the total token supply was reduced from 20 billion to 20 million, setting the exchange ratio at 1,000 ERD for 1 EGLD.

EGLD can be purchased on cryptocurrency exchanges such as Binance, OKEx, Bitfinex, and BitMax.

Mina Protocol (MINA)

Mina Protocol, formerly known as Coda Protocol, represents a groundbreaking approach to blockchain technology. Its primary aim is to reduce computational demands, enhancing efficiency and scalability for decentralized applications (DApps). Often touted as the world's lightest blockchain, Mina's unique feature is its ability to maintain a constant size despite increased usage while upholding a balance between security and decentralization. The rebranding from Coda Protocol to Mina occurred in October 2020.

Key to Mina's design is its exceptionally compact network size, a mere 22 KB, a stark contrast to Bitcoin's 300 GB blockchain.

Mina Protocol's Core Objective:

Mina aspires to create an efficient distributed payment system that empowers users to natively validate the platform starting from the genesis block. This concept is referred to as a "succinct blockchain" in their technical whitepaper.

Mina harnesses Zero-Knowledge Succinct Non-Interactive Arguments of Knowledge (zk-SNARKs), cryptographic proofs that authenticate information without revealing it. However, in larger networks, it can be impractical for users to trace the platform back to its genesis block. Therefore, Mina employs an incremental approach to compute zk-SNARKs focusing on only the most recent blocks. This way, end-users can verify the zk-SNARK-compressed proof, rather than an entire block's transaction history.

At the heart of the Mina protocol is MINA, its native currency, serving as both a utility coin and a medium of exchange.

How Mina Protocol Operates:

Mina shares similarities with Bitcoin in many aspects but differs significantly in how it handles transactions, incorporating the account model from Ethereum.

Where Bitcoin maintains a list of unspent coins, Ethereum's state comprises account balances. Mina introduces a prover, akin to a miner, ensuring that each block is committed to the state.

Mina employs the Ouroboros Samasika, a Proof of Stake (PoS) mechanism uniquely designed for succinct decentralized networks, facilitating a genesis block bootstrap.

Succinct blockchains encompass two key functions: verification and updating. Verification covers consensus, blockchain summaries, and blocks, while updating pertains to consensus and chain summaries.

In addition, the project utilizes a parallel scan state to optimize transaction processing speed, grouping unprocessed blocks and assigning the task to parallel provers.

Major Mina Protocol Participants:

Mina aims to revolutionize the typical blockchain landscape where verifiers, such as miners and stakers, along with light clients, often act as third parties when validating transactions.

Mina takes a distinct approach, introducing multiple participants, each assigned specific roles within the decentralized network.

The three primary roles encompass verifiers, block producers, and snarkers.

Verifiers:

Verifiers engage with zk-SNARKs, which play a vital role in certifying consensus information. Essentially, every Mina protocol user can act as a verifier, provided their devices can handle a 22 KB chain and a few milliseconds of processing time.

Block Producers:

Block producers, resembling stakers or miners, are responsible for earning block rewards and transaction fee payments. Notably, Mina's protocol does not penalize block producers. Users have the option to delegate their coins to these producers. In addition to bundling transactions into blocks, they are also tasked with generating SNARKs for previously committed trades.

Snarkers:

Snarkers, also known as provers, produce zk-SNARKs critical for transaction verification. Block producers compensate snarkers from the overall transaction fees they receive. However, snarkers must post bids to qualify for these fees, and the block producer using their SNARK incentivizes them. This arrangement creates a competitive economy among snarkers to produce cost-effective SNARKs.

Transaction Process on Mina:

The transaction process unfolds when a user initiates a transaction, sending it to the mempool, where valid but unconfirmed transactions gather. Subsequently, snarkers take the reins to create proofs or SNARKs. A block producer is then chosen to bundle these transactions into a block, scrutinizing the mempool for profitable transactions. The block producer selects a SNARK based on consensus rules. Notably, they evaluate the lowest-priced SNARK among the bids, and recent transactions have an updated SNARK order book. Once SNARKs are integrated into a block, it becomes a part of the chain, and snarked transactions are removed to maintain the protocol's constant size. The protocol's zk-SNARKs are updated, and the new block becomes an immutable part of the chain.

The Graph (GRT)

The Graph is an indexing protocol designed for querying data from networks like Ethereum and IPFS. It plays a pivotal role in numerous applications within the DeFi (Decentralized Finance) and broader Web3 ecosystem. The essence of The Graph lies in its ability to enable the creation and publication of open APIs, referred to as subgraphs. These subgraphs can be queried using GraphQL, facilitating the retrieval of blockchain data. A hosted service is currently available, simplifying the process for developers to initiate their work on The Graph, while a decentralized network is set to launch later.

Presently, The Graph extends support for indexing data from Ethereum, IPFS, and POA, with plans to incorporate more networks in the near future.

Key Features and Achievements:

The Graph boasts over 3,000 deployed subgraphs, a result of the collaborative efforts of thousands of developers. These subgraphs have been integrated into various DApps such as Uniswap, Synthetix, Aragon, AAVE, Gnosis, Balancer, Livepeer, DAOstack, Decentraland, and many more. Impressively, The Graph's usage has been steadily increasing at a rate of over 50% month-on-month, with over 7 billion queries recorded in September 2020.

The project has garnered a global community comprising more than 200 Indexer Nodes in the testnet and over 2,000 Curators in the Curator Program as of October 2020. To fund network development, The Graph raised funds from community members, strategic venture capitalists, and influential individuals within the blockchain community, including Coinbase Ventures, DCG, Framework, ParaFi Capital, CoinFund, DTC, Multicoin, Reciprocal Ventures, SPC, Tally Capital, and others. Additionally, The Graph Foundation successfully concluded a public GRT Sale, involving participants from 99 countries (excluding the U.S.). As of November 2020, The Graph had secured approximately $25 million in funding.

The Graph's team comprises professionals with extensive backgrounds from prominent organizations like the Ethereum Foundation, OpenZeppelin,

Decentraland, Orchid, MuleSoft (leading up to its IPO and acquisition by Salesforce), Puppet, Redhat, and Barclays. The initial co-founding team includes Yaniv Tal as the project lead, Brandon Ramirez as the research lead, and Jannis Pohlmann as the tech lead. These founders have engineering backgrounds and have collaborated for 5-8 years. Their vision for The Graph emerged from a previous project where they created immutable APIs and data access, employing the GraphQL query language.

Unique Aspects of The Graph:

The Graph is dedicated to bringing reliable decentralized public infrastructure to the mainstream. To ensure economic security for The Graph Network and data integrity during queries, participants engage with the Graph Token (GRT). GRT is a work token that Indexers, Curators, and Delegators lock up to provide indexing and curating services. It will be an ERC-20 token on the Ethereum blockchain, allocating resources within the network. Active participants can earn income proportional to their contributions and GRT stake. Indexers receive indexing rewards and query fees, Curators receive a share of query fees, and Delegators earn a portion of the income generated by the Indexer they delegate to.

Circulation of GRT Tokens:

At the mainnet launch, the total supply of GRT tokens will be 10 billion, with an initial circulating supply of approximately 1,245,666,867 GRT. The issuance of new tokens, primarily through indexing rewards, begins at a rate of 3% annually. The specifics of token economics and distribution are detailed in official documents.

The Graph has established an open data layer atop blockchains. Indexers can operate their Ethereum archive nodes to run the Graph Node, or they can utilize node operators like Infura or Alchemy. The structure allows any analytics company to create applications for querying subgraph data that The Graph indexes. Subgraphs serve as open APIs, streamlining the process of extracting data from the blockchain efficiently and seamlessly.

The Sandbox (SAND)

Released in 2011 by Pixowl, "The Sandbox" is a blockchain-based virtual world that allows users to create, buy, and sell digital assets in the form of a game. Combining the strengths of decentralized autonomous organizations (DAOs) and NFTs, The Sandbox creates a decentralized platform for a thriving gaming community.

According to the official white paper, the main mission of The Sandbox platform is to successfully introduce blockchain technology into mainstream gaming (real-time action and strategy games). The platform focuses on facilitating a creative "play-to-earn" model, which allows users to be both creators and players at the same time. The Sandbox leverages the power of blockchain technology with the introduction of the SAND utility token, which facilitates transactions on the platform.

Who are the founders of The Sandbox?

Arthur Madrid is a co-founder and the CEO of Pixowl and is one of the driving forces behind The Sandbox. He graduated with a degree in economics from the Université Paris Dauphine in 2000. Madrid's professional career started as a consultant for Eurogroup Consulting France, but he soon found his entrepreneurial spirit. In 2001, he founded 1-Click Media, which was later acquired by Ipercast.

Sebastien Borget is also a co-founder of Pixowl and serves as the company's COO. He graduated with a degree in computer systems networking and telecommunications from the National Telecommunications Institute in 2007. His professional career began as a project lead for 1-Click Media and since then, Arthur Madrid and Sebastien Borget have been a business duo. They founded Pixowl in 2011 and are constantly working on projects together.

What makes The Sandbox unique?

The Sandbox is a unique platform because it introduces blockchain technology to the world of gaming. The gaming industry is a huge untapped market in terms of blockchain technology adoption, and Pixowl saw this in 2011. By creating a universe where players can create and collect blockchain-based assets, The Sandbox aims to revolutionize the market. It is creating a position for itself in the global gaming market.

By focusing on user-generated content, The Sandbox creates a grid of engaged players who contribute to the further development of the platform. Not only that, by introducing the SAND token, The Sandbox promotes decentralized governance and allows users to share their opinions and ideas about the development of the project. Thanks to evolving technology, decentralized governance is becoming an essential element in blockchain-based projects.

The company was launched with great success and attracted support and investment from many big names in the gaming industry such as Atari, Helix, and CryptoKitties.

How many The Sandbox (SAND) coins are in circulation?

There is a maximum and total supply of 3,000,000,000 SAND. Currently, approximately 680,266,194 SAND are in active circulation, representing 23% of the total available supply as of March 2021.

Of the total token offering, approximately 25.82% was allocated to the company's reserve. Another 17.18% was allocated for the initial token sale. The founders and team members secured approximately 31% of the total offering distributed among themselves. About 12% of the total offering was allocated for an exclusive sale of Binance Launchpad and another 10% was dedicated as a reward to advisors for the project.

The Sandbox is enjoying increased interest from investors and users alike. More and more exchanges are offering SAND trading. Binance has the highest volume of SAND to BUSD trading (where BUSD, or Binance USD, is a stable currency with 1:1 backing to USD, issued by Binance, approved and regulated by the New York State Department of Financial Services).

Other options for the SAND market include Uniswap (V2), Gate.io, and LATOKEN.

Decentraland (MANA)

Decentraland (MANA) defines itself as a virtual reality platform powered by the Ethereum blockchain. It allows users to create, experience, and generate revenue from content and applications.

In this virtual world, users buy plots of land which they can later navigate, build on, and generate revenue from.

Decentraland launched after a $24 million Initial Coin Offering (ICO) in 2017. The virtual world released its closed beta version in 2019 and opened to the public in February 2020. Since then, users have created a wide range of experiences in the LAND parcels, including interactive games, expansive 3D scenes, and a variety of other interactive experiences.

Decentraland uses two tokens: MANA and LAND. MANA is an ERC-20 token that must be burned to obtain NFT ERC-721 LAND (ERC-721 is a free, open standard that describes how to create non-fungible or unique tokens on the Ethereum blockchain). MANA can also be used to purchase a range of avatars, wearables, names, and more on the Decentraland marketplace.

Who are the founders of Decentraland?

Decentraland was founded by Ariel Meilich and Esteban Ordano. Both have stepped down from important positions in the project, but still work with Decentraland as consultants.

Ariel Meilich previously held the role of Project Lead at Decentraland between 2017 and 2020. He is an entrepreneur who has founded several other startups, including an online translation agency and a CRM platform. He also worked as an analyst at Charles River Ventures, a prominent Silicon Valley venture capital firm.

On the other hand, Esteban Ordano is the former Technology Lead at Decentraland. He has a long and varied history in the cryptocurrency space, working as a software engineer at BitPay, Inc., a consultant for Matic Network, and briefly running his own smart contracts development company known as Smart Contract Solutions.

Esteban Ordano is also credited as a co-founder of Zeppelin Solutions, an established blockchain technology infrastructure company.

Although Ariel Meilich and Esteban Ordano are no longer leading the project, the development of Decentraland is still ongoing, with efforts now being directed by the newly established Decentraland Foundation.

What makes the Decentraland project unique?

The Decentraland project has been created for content creators, businesses, and individuals looking for a new artistic medium, business opportunity, or source of entertainment.

In total, the Decentraland world is divided into 90,601 individual LAND parcels, each represented by an NFT ERC-721. Each LAND is exactly 16m x 16m (256 square meters) and can be found at a specific coordinate in the Metaverse.

Although LAND holders are free to develop their land into whatever they choose, much of the Metaverse is broadly divided into several areas, each of which has a different size and theme. LAND parcels in areas created through individual sales for MANA cannot be negotiated.

Decentraland is also one of the growing projects that use a decentralized autonomous organization (DAO) structure for governance decisions. As a result, MANA token holders control how the Decentraland world behaves by proposing and voting on policy updates, specifics of upcoming LAND auctions, and types of content allowed in the Metaverse.

In addition to creative outlets, many Decentraland users generate income from their plots of land through leasing, advertising, and paid experiences.

Similarly, other users generate income by creating and selling items in the Decentraland marketplace and receiving MANA.

How many Decentraland (MANA) coins are in circulation?

As of January 2021, 1.49 billion MANA tokens were in circulation. This equates to approximately 68% of the current total supply of 2.19 billion MANA tokens.

The initial total offer was set at 2.8 billion MANA, but has been reduced as more than 600 million MANA have been burned as a result of the LAND auctions.

There are also a number of other burn mechanisms to further reduce the circulating supply of MANA, including the burning of 2.5% of MANA in Decentraland market trades.

The MANA token was originally designed to rise to reach an inflation rate of 8% in the first year, falling gradually over time to reduce the rate of inflation. But inflation is currently off. According to Decentraland, there are no plans to start inflation "until needed."

In total, 40% of the MANA offering was sold during the 2017 Initial Coin Offering (ICO). In addition, 20% was reserved for community incentives, 20% went to the development team and other initial contributors, and the remaining 20% was held by Decentraland.

MANA currently benefits from excellent liquidity and can be bought, traded, or sold on around 100 different exchange platforms. As of January 2021, Binance, OKEx, and Coinbase Pro are among the most liquid exchanges for MANA.

Helium (HNT)

Helium (HNT) is a decentralized network powered by a blockchain for Internet of Things (IoT) devices.

The main Helium network, which was released in July 2019, allows low-power wireless devices to communicate with each other and send data over its network of nodes.

The nodes come in the form of so-called Hotspots, which are a combination of a wireless gateway and a blockchain mining device. Thus, users operating nodes mine and earn rewards on Helium's native cryptocurrency token, HNT.

Helium aims to prepare IoT communications for the future by identifying shortcomings in the current infrastructure.

Who are the founders of Helium?

Helium's three co-founders Amir Haleem, Shawn Fanning, and Sean Carey started the company in 2013.

Haleem has an active background in eSports and game development. Fanning is best known for developing Napster, the music sharing service, which was one of the first mainstream peer-to-peer (P2P) internet services in the late 1990s.

Meanwhile, Carey held several development roles prior to Helium, which included ad optimization company Where, which was acquired by PayPal.

The Helium team now consists of members who the company says have experience in "radio, hardware, manufacturing, distributed systems, peer-to-peer, and blockchain technologies."

What makes Helium unique?

Helium aims to improve the communication capabilities of wireless Internet of Things (IoT) devices. In 2013, the infrastructure around IoT was still in its infancy, but developers wanted to add decentralization to their offering, hence they refer to it as "The People's Network" in the official literature.

Its main appeal is to device owners and those interested in the IoT space, giving financial incentives to provide further outreach opportunities.

Network participants buy a Hotspot – a combination of wireless gateway and mining – or create their own. Each Hotspot provides network coverage in a specific radius and also mines Helium's native token, HNT.

The network works with Proof of Coverage, a new consensus algorithm based on the HoneyBadger BFT (Byzantine Fault Tolerant) protocol, which allows nodes in a network to reach consensus when the quality of the connection is highly variable.

How much Helium (HNT) is in circulation?

Approximately, mining periods of 30 to 60 minutes unlock rewards that are distributed according to a variable growth pattern.

Helium explains that in the beginning, node owners will accumulate more HNT tokens to build network infrastructure, while later, it will be more advantageous to transfer device data. This adaptation mechanism for token distribution is expected to last for about 20 years.

As of the beginning of October 2020, 48,712,218 HNT are in circulation. When the token was released, the supply was zero, with no pre-mining.

HNT is a tradable token that has been available on major exchanges since October 2020, such as Binance.

Hedera (HBAR)

Hedera is a public network designed for decentralized applications (DApps) and is committed to sustainability and efficiency. It differs from traditional blockchains by using a unique consensus algorithm called hashgraph, which is known for its fast transaction processing, cost-effectiveness, and scalability.

Hedera issued its native utility token, HBAR, through an initial coin offering (ICO) in 2018. HBAR plays a dual role within the network. First, it powers various services such as smart contracts, file storage, and regular transactions. Second, it's used to secure the network through staking.

The platform offers several core services, including the Consensus Service (HCS), which allows consensus timestamping and order negotiation, and the Hedera Token Service (HTS) for token creation and management.

One key feature is the Gossip-about-Gossip protocol, where nodes share data to achieve consensus. Unlike traditional blockchains, Hedera's hashgraph approach merges all transaction branches, ensuring none are discarded in the consensus process.

HBAR is used to pay for network services, transaction fees, in-app payments, and micropayments. Hedera is governed by a decentralized council, which makes important decisions regarding pricing, software updates, and wealth management.

Regarding circulation, there's a maximum supply of 50 billion HBAR tokens. As of January 2021, nearly seven billion HBAR tokens were in circulation, equivalent to approximately 14% of the total supply. Hedera publishes reports detailing the release of additional tokens.

The project founders and senior executives were granted varying amounts of HBAR tokens, with vesting periods defined for each group. According to an economics whitepaper, an estimated 17.03 billion HBAR tokens are expected to be in circulation by 2025, equivalent to around 34% of the total supply.

Aptos (APT)

Aptos is a blockchain platform designed to bring mainstream adoption to web3 and facilitate a thriving ecosystem of decentralized applications (DApps). This Layer 1 Proof-of-Stake (PoS) blockchain employs a unique smart contract programming language called Move, developed independently by Meta (formerly Facebook)'s Diem blockchain engineers, using the Rust programming language.

One of Aptos's key features is its impressive transaction throughput, with a theoretical capacity exceeding 150,000 transactions per second (tps) made possible through parallel execution. For comparison, Ethereum's mainnet typically handles around 12 to 15 tps.

Aptos's innovation lies in its parallel execution engine, known as Block-STM, which employs a byzantine fault-tolerant (BFT) PoS consensus mechanism. While most blockchains process transactions sequentially, risking bottlenecks from a single failed transaction or high network demand, Aptos processes all transactions simultaneously and validates them afterward. Failed transactions can be either re-executed or aborted, thanks to the blockchain's software transactional memory libraries that detect and manage conflicts.

Moreover, Aptos leverages the Move programming language to create smart contracts. Move offers several advantages over Solidity, Ethereum's smart contract language, including easily verifiable blockchain commands, private key modification, and the modular design of the Aptos platform.

Aptos's flexibility and upgradeability, combined with horizontal throughput scalability through its natively implemented sharding feature, enhance the user experience and allow for the exploration of new use cases.

In terms of its native currency, APT is the token of the Aptos blockchain. It was initially released with a total supply of 1 billion tokens. As of the latest data, 130 million APT tokens are in circulation. These tokens are distributed as follows: Community (51.02%); Core Contributors (19.00%); Foundation (16.50%); Investors (13.48%).

The Community allocation is divided with approximately 80% held by the Aptos Foundation and the remaining portion by Aptos Labs. Over the next decade, these tokens will be gradually unlocked to support community growth and Aptos Foundation initiatives.

Investors and core contributors are subject to a four-year vesting schedule starting from the mainnet launch. Additionally, Aptos initiated a token airdrop of 20 million APT tokens to early testnet users on October 19, 2022.

Lastly, Aptos Bridge, an on-chain user application protocol developed by LayerZero Labs, was introduced on October 19, 2022. This blockchain bridge enables users to transfer Ethereum (ETH), USDC, and USDT from various other blockchains such as Ethereum, BNB Chain, Polygon, Avalanche, and Optimism to the Aptos network, enhancing interoperability between different blockchain ecosystems.

Audius (AUDIO)

Audius is a decentralized music streaming protocol originally built on the Proof of Activity (PoA) network. It is a consensus algorithm for the blockchain that is a combination of Proof of Work and Proof of Stake. It is used to ensure that all transactions that take place on the blockchain are authentic and all miners come to a consensus. Audius now lives in Solana. Audius was released to correct the inefficiencies of the music industry, which is plagued by opaque ownership of music rights and middlemen standing between artists and their audiences.

Audius aims to align the interests of artists, fans, and node operators through its platform, powered by the native AUDIO token. Artists can upload music, which is stored and distributed by content and discovery nodes, while fans can listen to the music for free. Currently, Audius rewards content creators through rewards such as appearing on weekly trend lists. In the future, it plans to incorporate stablecoins for artists who offer paid content, as well as artist tokens that give fans access to exclusive content. It may also partner with platforms like Rally, which is a platform for creators and their communities to create their own independent digital economies.

Who are the founders of Audius?

Audius was founded in 2018 by Roneil Rumburg and Forrest Browning, two California-based entrepreneurs. Roneil Rumburg is a graduate of Stanford University. He founded Kleiner Perkins, a venture capital firm that invests in blockchain and AI companies. Forrest Browning, also a Stanford graduate, is on the Forbes 30 Under 30 list and is co-founder of StacksWare, an enterprise data center management platform. The team is rounded out by 21 other employees and is supported by a number of other prominent names, including Deadmau5, a popular electronic music producer; Adam Goldberg, co-founder and CEO of Stanford Crypto; and Bing Gordon, co-founder of EA Games.

What makes Audius unique?

The Audius ecosystem consists of four main components: artists, fans, content nodes, and discovery nodes.

Artists publish content on the Audius universal content portal. They can do so at no cost. Music is streamed at 320 kbps, comparable to Spotify and Google Play Music standards. Due to the decentralized nature of Audius, there is no copyright protection, although the protocol operates on a community-supervised arbitration system. Artists can use Audius to experiment or share bonus tracks. The platform plans to include artist tokens to facilitate revenue generation, provided artists stake on AUDIO. Artists can also participate in programs that reward the most popular artists with free tokens.

Fans can listen to tracks for free. In the future, they may be given the opportunity to stake on AUDIO to participate in the development of artists on the platform. They can also showcase their verified NFTs through the platform and earn various badges. Content nodes maintain content availability in AudSP, the native extension of the InterPlanetary File System (IPFS) on the platform. An artist's client selects a set of these nodes to automatically make the artist's content available on the artist's behalf, while fan clients retrieve content, submit proofs, and request keys for content nodes. Artists can also manage their own content nodes and maintain more control over their content distribution. The content ledger maintains a record and a single source of truth for all actions in the protocol.

In other words, they enable users to find new content and act as registrars of its registry data on the platform.

How many Audius (AUDIO) coins are in circulation?

The total AUDIO supply is 1 billion tokens, with 411 million AUDIO tokens currently in circulation. The annual inflation rate is 7%. 50 million AUDIO tokens distributed to the top 10 artists and fans, with 75% going to artists based on number of streams. The token distribution is as follows: 23% to predefined rewards and airdrops, 36% to investors, and 41% to founders and the protocol itself.

The token is designed for three main purposes: network security, unlocking access to functions, and acting as a governance symbol.

Tokens can be staked as collateral for value-added services. Node operators can also stake AUDIO to secure the network and execute the protocol. Each token also receives some governance weight and influences the future of the protocol.

AUDIO is available on Binance, Uniswap (V2), BitStamp, and Gate.io.

NEAR Protocol (NEAR)

The NEAR protocol is a Level 1 blockchain designed as a cloud platform that is community-driven. It eliminates some of the limitations that plague competing blockchains, such as slow transaction speeds, low performance, and poor interoperability. This provides the ideal environment for DApps and creates a platform for developers that is user-friendly. For example, NEAR uses account names that are human-readable, as opposed to crypto wallet addresses that are common in Ethereum. NEAR also introduces unique solutions to scalability problems and has its own consensus mechanism, called "Doomslug."

The NEAR protocol is created by the NEAR Collective, its community that updates the source code and issues updates to the ecosystem. Its stated goal is to build a platform that is "secure enough to manage high-value assets like money or identity, and performant enough to make them useful for everyday people."

Flux, which we talked about earlier, a protocol that allows developers to create markets based on assets, commodities, and real-world events, as well as Mintbase, an NFT minting platform, are examples of projects built on the NEAR Protocol.

Who are the founders of the NEAR Protocol (NEAR)?

NEAR Protocol was founded by Erik Trautman, an entrepreneur with Wall Street experience and founder of Viking Education. The co-founders were Illia Polosukhin, who has more than ten years of industry experience, including three years at Google, and Alexander Skidanov, a computer scientist who worked at Microsoft and joined memSQL, where he became director of technical development. NEAR Protocol has an extensive team of experienced programmers that includes several gold medalists and winners of the International Collegiate Programming Contest (ICPC). The team claims to have people with experience in building some of the unique sharded systems at scale that exist in the real world, a solution the protocol is pursuing to improve blockchain scalability.

What makes the NEAR Protocol (NEAR) unique?

NEAR uses Nightshade's technology to massively improve trading performance. Nightshade is a variant of sharding, in which individual sets of validators process transactions in parallel on multiple sharded chains, improving the overall capacity of the blockchain. Unlike "normal" sharding, the shards in Nightshade produce a fraction of the next block, called a "chunk." In this way, the NEAR Protocol is able to achieve up to 100,000 transactions per second and near-instantaneous transaction finalization at a rate of one second per block, while keeping transaction fees near zero.

The NEAR protocol also improves the complex process of integrating other blockchains by having human-readable addresses and creating decentralized applications that have a flow of records similar to what users have already experienced. In addition, it provides developers with modular elements (modules are pieces of code) for programming, helping them to more quickly start various projects, such as contracts or NFTs.

How many NEAR Protocol (NEAR) coins are in circulation?

The total supply of NEAR is 1 billion tokens, according to the following breakdown:

17,2% – Grants to the Community
11,4% – Operating grants
10% – Foundation
11,7% – Early Ecosystem
14% – Key Contributors
17,6% – Supporters

6,1% – Small Supporters

12% – Sale in the Community

The NEAR Protocol released its mainnet on 22 April 2020 with 1 billion NEAR tokens created at the beginning. 5% of the additional commission is issued each year to support the network as seasonal rewards, of which 90% goes to validators (4.5% in total) and 10% to the protocol fund (0.5% in total). 30% of transaction commissions are paid as rebates on contracts that interact with a transaction, while the remaining 70% is burned. NEAR is used for the following: transaction processing and data storage charges, execution of validation nodes in the network via NEAR staking, and governance votes to determine how network resources are allocated.

NEAR is available on Binance, Huobi Global, Mandala Exchange, and OKEx.

OKB (OKB)

OKB is a cryptocurrency released by the OK Blockchain Foundation in partnership with the prominent Maltese cryptocurrency exchange, OKEx. Known for being one of the world's largest exchanges, OKEx ranks third in liquidity and fourth in trading volume at the moment of writing this. It offers a wide variety of trading pairs and features. While it shares some similarities with the cryptocurrency exchange giant Binance, it distinguishes itself through offerings like its cloud mining service and a strong focus on options trading.

At its core, OKB serves as the utility token for OKEx, granting users access to the exchange's special features and benefits. This token is used to calculate and pay trading fees, offer users the opportunity to participate in voting and governance activities on the platform, and even rewards users for holding OKB.

OKEx has rapidly risen to become a global leader in cryptocurrency trading since its launch in 2017. The platform originated as an offshoot from the original OKCoin platform, which had been operational in China since 2013. OKCoin now primarily facilitates fiat-to-crypto exchanges, while OKEx specializes in crypto trading. It boasts a built-in API for algorithmic trading, a multi-currency wallet, and features for margin trading.

Key Figures at OKEx:

Jay Hao has been the CEO of OKEx from the start and continues to lead the company. With a background in technology and engineering, Hao has closely followed developments in the blockchain industry, particularly in the realm of blockchain-based applications for video streaming and mobile gaming. Before joining OKEx, he accumulated two decades of experience in the semiconductor industry, making significant contributions to product development and management.

Another notable member of OKEx's management team is Mingxing "Star" Xu. He founded OKCoin in China in 2013, establishing himself as a prominent figure in the industry. In 2017, Xu co-founded OKEx in Malta as a separate legal entity. Today, he serves as the CEO of the OK Group.

OKB's Role in the OKEx Ecosystem:

The OKB token plays a pivotal role within the OKEx ecosystem. It enables users to receive discounts on their transactions, with discounts of up to 40% based on the number of OKB tokens held. OKEx classifies users into two categories: regular and VIP. Regular users are assigned a level based on their OKB holdings, while VIP users are ranked according to their trading volume. Discounts are updated daily, providing users with incentives based on their respective levels.

OKB is also instrumental in enabling passive income for platform members and is utilized in OKEx Earn, a project that assists users in generating income from their assets. Another function of the OKB token is its involvement in fund allocation on the OKEx Jumpstart platform, which is accessible following registration on the site. Sales are conducted through MixTrust.

Furthermore, OKB serves as the native asset on the OKExChain, OKEx's blockchain, and supports spot trading, derivatives trading, and the simultaneous development of scalable applications. The layered architecture of the OKB blockchain enhances consensus times, scalability, and security.

To add value to OKB and enhance its appeal to holders, OKEx conducts regular token burns every three months, with details of the burns published on the official website. For these burns, OKEx allocates 30% of its commission fee income. Additionally, welcome bonuses are provided to new users.

OKB Token Circulation:

The OKB token shares some similarities with Binance Coin (BNB) as a global utility token. 50% of the service fee income is distributed among token holders based on their OKB balance. OKB holders enjoy various privileges, including the right to participate in platform voting, invest, and trade on OKEx.

The current market includes 1 billion OKB tokens, allocated as follows:

40% for Founders & Project

10% for Investors

50% for AirDrops & Rewards

The Meme Coins and Their Function

As the name suggests, meme coins are a type of cryptocurrency inspired by memes, interesting or funny ideas recorded from an image, video or other media. Dogecoin and Shiba Inu are two of the most popular and well-known examples.

Meme coins are cryptocurrencies, such as Bitcoin or Ethereum. But, unlike these tokens, meme coins are usually designed around a joke, an interesting or funny idea captured in an image, video or other medium. Like the memes they are based on, memecoins are designed to go viral and be shared.

Dogecoin, one of the biggest meme coins on the market, was originally created as a joke to mock Bitcoin and other major cryptocurrencies. Its developers, software engineers Billy Markus and Jackson Palmer, did not intend to create a currency for real use, but just for fun. This is also true of most meme coins. Unlike utility tokens, meme coins are generally not used for participating in a DAO, staking, or making purchases in a particular ecosystem. They exist only to be exchanged and for those who want to make fun of them.

What is the value of these coins?

Simple cryptocurrencies, in general, suffer from more drastic changes in value than traditional currencies. But at the end of the day, because of the project behind them, they always have value. However, the same is not the case with meme coins. These take volatility to a completely different level, with no real value, and can be shut down as a project after a few hours.

One of the reasons that meme coins undergo such extreme changes in value is the way they are designed. Unlike fiat currencies and most cryptocurrencies, meme coins often have an uncapped supply, meaning there is no limit to how many of them can exist.

The value of any meme currency is largely determined by how viral it has become. When Elon Musk and Mark Cuban promoted Dogecoin, its value skyrocketed. But once the hype ended, it fell just as quickly.

Some popular meme coins are Dogecoin, Shiba Inu, Dogelon Mars, Floki Inu, and Baby Doge Coin.

In general, meme coins are not designed as a utility token, but exclusively for trading. They are highly volatile and subject to extreme changes in value over very short periods of time. They often have an uncapped supply, and their prices are determined by the trend surrounding the token, but usually have a very low value per token.

However, cryptocurrency investors should not write off meme coins as if they are completely worthless. Fortunes have been made and lost in the meme coin space. Also, Dogecoin and Shiba Inu as a project, although they started out as a joke, eventually made it to the top 20 and stayed there.

Later, because of the success of these two meme coins, they started to do more substantial projects around this type of coin. So, they may have started as a joke, but eventually they gained a lot of value and are used by big investors around the world.

The meme coin is known for its large price increase. One can become a millionaire in a few days with $100. Very few investments can offer this kind of quick return. And this is why investors should not completely ignore meme coins, even if they are only a small part of their investment strategy and have a higher risk.

The key to making money from meme coins is to know what's going to go viral before it does. By staying aware of current and future trends, meme coins can be an incredibly valuable investment. This is especially true because their value is so low, allowing investors to buy a significant amount for a minimal amount of money.

For example, I remember that in the summer of 2021 I received a tweet on my mobile phone with Elon Musk singing about the Baby Doge Coin. Although I saw it within the first hour of it going up, the price had already gone up several times. Within 72 hours that price had gone up 8 times. A lot of people bought when they saw the price go up. But after a while the value started to fall, which means that most people did not make a profit from this investment. So this makes meme coins a high risk investment.

Even if you choose to never invest in meme coins because of the high risk, they are an important part of today's cryptocurrency market. It's something you should be aware of because they definitely influence other currencies to a great extent.

The Function of the Meme Coins

In the past, creating a meme coin required some technical knowledge. Now, however, apps and websites have been developed that make this job very easy. While this is good because it helps more people work in this field, it also allows scammers to take advantage of less-experienced investors.

Meme coins work like any other cryptocurrency. More specifically, they have appeared on blockchains that use smart contracts, such as Ethereum. Today, there are thousands of meme coins on these blockchains, and many more are created every hour.

Buying meme coins is no more difficult than buying Bitcoin or Ethereum, but many meme coins are not available on major exchanges like Binance and Coinbase. That's the trick with them, as every time a large exchange, like one of the above, adds a meme coin to their platform, its value goes through the roof and beyond. Meme coins can be bought, sold, and traded just like any other type of cryptocurrency on the platforms that accept this currency.

Unfortunately, most coin memes don't provide a clear utility for anything. Remember, they are not designed for use in DAO or as a staking token.

You can look for opportunities to buy when a meme coin is at a low price and sell it when it is at a high price. It is more of an investment than something you are going to use.

Security in Meme Coins

If you have read everything written here about meme coins, then you probably already know that they are not the most stable investment. Their high supply and volatility make them an inherently riskier investment. While Elon Musk (or some other celebrity) could tweet about a meme coin and skyrocket in value tomorrow, the entire project could just as easily disappear in less than a week and no one could ever refund your money.

Remember, meme coins are based on memes and jokes on the internet. And as such, they share many characteristics with them, including the potential to go viral or be overcome very quickly.

However, it is possible to safely invest in meme coins and earn an incredible amount of money. It just takes familiarity with the subject, good information, and some basic knowledge of how common scams in this field are done.

Always make sure that a third party trusted company has checked the meme coin project, such as Binance, which has done it with Shiba Inu and Dogecoin. Many times, such companies check such projects before uploading them. If they have uploaded them to their trading platforms, then it is almost certain that the meme coin has passed all the checks.

Be careful with any currency where developers hold most of its tokens. Ideally, no one person or organization should control more than 50% of the total token supply. If they have more than that, then they can move the market as they wish and will have the power to take most of the money and disappear.

There are many platforms that check and show us whether a project is a scam or not. Of course, they don't say outright that something is a scam or not, they just say that there are more chances of it being a scam or less chances of it being a scam. No one can tell you for sure if something is a scam or not, as we've already seen some of the bigger projects like Terra Luna disappear. One such audit site is www.bscheck.eu. You can put in the contract from the project you want to audit and it will show you the most basic data that is important. It will also show you whether or not that project could be a scam.

Dogecoin (DOGE)

Dogecoin (DOGE) is based on the popular online meme "doge" and has a dog of the popular hunting dog breed from Japan, Shiba Inu, in its logo. The creators of Dogecoin envisioned it as a fun cryptocurrency with no particularly serious meaning that would have more appeal than Bitcoin's core audience, because it was based on the meme of a dog. The open source digital currency was created by Billy Markus and Jackson Palmer. The most significant fact about this cryptocurrency is that the well-known Tesla CEO, Elon Musk, has posted in several tweets on social media that Dogecoin is his favorite currency, which has given it great value. Although it had no use until then, it has since become one of the favorite cryptocurrencies of many.

You can sell or buy Dogecoin on any exchange that offers the digital currency, store it on an exchange or in a Dogecoin wallet, and give it to any communities that accept Dogecoin. It is now available on almost all exchanges, as it is one of the most well-known cryptocurrencies, having spent a long time in the Top 10 cryptocurrencies.

The success of Dogecoin is closely intertwined with Elon Musk's passion for it. Musk began tweeting about Dogecoin in early 2021, sharing a Lion King meme with DOGE. This started a crazy rally for DOGE.

Eventually, DOGE crashed after some time despite Musk's promises. In the following months, Musk seemed to lose interest and DOGE's price fell more than 70% from its all-time high. However, Musk still attributes power to Dogecoin, as evidenced by occasional tweets and wanting to use it to make donations to his own projects, such as Spacex.

In 2014, a non-profit foundation was created by members of the Dogecoin team to provide support, advocacy, trademark protection, and governance for the meme coin. However, the foundation disbanded over time and was relaunched in 2021, adding some of the most experienced people in the industry.

Of course, this group now has some of the biggest names in the cryptocurrency world, and that is what gives hope to those who invest in this currency. The advisory team consists of Dogecoin founder Billy Markus, the project's lead developer Max Keller, Ethereum founder Vitalik Buterin, and Elon Musk represented by his family office head Jared Birchall.

Shiba Inu (SHIB)

The Shiba Inu coin was created anonymously in August 2020 under the pseudonym "Ryoshi." The meme coin quickly gained value as the coin's cute charm had attracted a community of investors, coupled with headlines and tweets from celebrities like Elon Musk and Vitalik Buterin, but also because they thought it was the next Dogecoin that would make them millionaires.

Shiba Inu aimed to be the equivalent of Dogecoin, but based on Ethereum. Shiba Inu and the SHIB token are part of a series of dog-themed cryptocurrencies, including Baby Doge Coin (BabyDoge), Dogecoin (DOGE), Jindo Inu (JIND), Alaska Inu (LAS), and Alaskan Malamute Token (LASM). Most of these have no real value except for the hope they give some people that they might be the next big thing that will make them millionaires.

It's now working on its own metaverse game, and that shows that as a project in general is getting attention. It's also working on a lot of real products that will create real value for cryptocurrency in the future.

There are currently, according to Coinmarketcap, 549,063,278,876,302 SHIB tokens. No more SHIB tokens can be created through mining or any other option. The original total supply was 1 quadrillion coins, but the remainder was burned, reducing the total supply significantly and increasing the price of each coin.

There are other tokens made to support Shiba Inu, such as Leash and Bone. On Shibaswap, one can stake their SHIB tokens and get either Leash or Bone. The platform is built with a lot of humor; for example, you can "bury your tokens," which is a term for staking your tokens. All of these, aside from the nice title they have been given, are ways in which you can leverage your SHIB tokens on their platform.

SHIB is now available on all major exchanges. It is the second largest meme coin in the world at the moment and has attracted many investors who believe it will be the currency that will prevail in the future.

Pepe (PEPE)

PEPE is a deflationary memecoin that was launched on the Ethereum blockchain. This cryptocurrency pays homage to the iconic Pepe the Frog internet meme, originally created by Matt Furie, which gained prominence in the early 2000s.

The primary objective of this project is to tap into the popularity of meme coins, following in the footsteps of coins like Shiba Inu and Dogecoin. PEPE aims to establish itself as one of the leading meme-based cryptocurrencies. It stands out by adopting a no-tax policy and openly acknowledging its lack of utility, emphasizing its pure and straightforward memecoin nature.

In the late April to May period of 2023, PEPE experienced a remarkable surge, driving its market capitalization to a peak of $1.6 billion at one point. This surge led to early holders becoming millionaires and attracted a dedicated community of like-minded enthusiasts. This surge is often referred to as a "memecoin season," inspiring other memecoins to experience rapid price pumps and equally significant price drops. The future success of PEPE and other memecoins remains uncertain, but many believers are optimistic, particularly in anticipation of the upcoming Bitcoin halving cycle.

The PEPE project follows a three-phase roadmap. Phase one includes listing on CoinMarketCap and generating buzz on Twitter. Phase two involves listing on centralized exchanges (CEXs), while phase three includes securing listings on "tier 1" exchanges and what the team describes as a "meme takeover."

Who Are the Founders of Pepe?

As of now, the identities of the PEPE founders remain undisclosed, a common practice in the cryptocurrency realm. Despite limited information about the team behind the project, they have effectively harnessed social media platforms such as Twitter to promote their meme coin and cultivate a community of meme coin enthusiasts.

How Many PEPE Coins Are in Circulation?

PEPE employs a redistribution system designed to reward long-term stakers, providing them with incentives to remain committed to the project. This strategy fosters coin stability by encouraging users to hold the token rather than selling it quickly. Additionally, PEPE implements a burning mechanism that permanently removes a portion of the coins from circulation on a regular basis, with the aim of maintaining scarcity, even with a maximum supply of 420,690,000,000,000 coins.

Out of the maximum supply, 93.1% were allocated to the liquidity pool on Uniswap, where LP tokens were burned, and the deployer contract was sent to a null address. The remaining 6.9% is held in a multi-signature wallet, designated for future listings on centralized exchanges, bridges, and liquidity pools.

Cryptocurrency Exchanges

Author's Note: Evaluating Cryptocurrency Exchanges

As we delve into the exciting world of cryptocurrencies, it is essential to understand that the information presented in this chapter is based on my personal assessment and the available data at the time of writing. Cryptocurrency exchanges are dynamic entities in a constantly evolving financial landscape, and while I may have my preferences, it's important to emphasize that the best choice for you may depend on various factors and your individual needs.

In compiling my list of recommended exchanges, I have considered a range of criteria, including safety, services, and regulatory compliance. These recommendations are guided by my own experience and research, as well as the desire to provide readers with exchanges that have maintained a strong track record for security and reliability. I have also taken into account the status of these exchanges with regards to financial regulators.

However, it is crucial to recognize that the cryptocurrency market is subject to rapid change, and new developments, regulations, or security issues can impact the standing of any exchange. Moreover, every individual's requirements, risk tolerance, and trading preferences are unique. What suits one person may not be the best fit for another.

Therefore, I strongly advise all readers to conduct their own research and due diligence when choosing a cryptocurrency exchange. Consider your investment goals, level of experience, desired features, and local regulations. While I have ranked the following exchanges based on my criteria, the ultimate decision should be yours, tailored to your specific circumstances.

Cryptocurrencies are a powerful and innovative financial asset, but they require a responsible approach. Your choice of exchange plays a vital role in your crypto journey, and by making an informed decision, you can contribute to a safer and more prosperous experience in the cryptocurrency world.

Happy reading, and may your cryptocurrency endeavors be both rewarding and secure.

OKX Exchange

OKX is an innovative cryptocurrency exchange with advanced financial services. It is one of the world's leading cryptocurrency exchanges by trading volume. It serves millions of users in more than 100 countries. It provides services such as: spot trading, margin trading, futures, options, perpetual swaps trading, DeFi, lending, and mining. It used to be called OKEx. Now you will only find it as OKX, but it is the same company.

OKX is adopting blockchain to build the next generation financial ecosystem. It seeks to eliminate financial barriers, evolve the global economy, and change the world for the better. Security is its top priority. OKX provides a secure, reliable, and stable environment for cryptocurrency transactions via web and mobile apps.

OKB is the token of the OKX utility, which allows users to access the special features of the exchange. The token is used to calculate and pay transaction commissions, reward users for owning OKB, and provide users with access for platform governance and voting. It was released by the OK Blockchain Foundation and the OKX exchange.

The OKX exchange is one of the largest in the world. It currently ranks third in liquidity, fourth in trading volume, and provides a wide selection of trading pairs. It is similar in many aspects to cryptocurrency exchange giant Binance, but there are a few key differences. The OKX platform has its own cloud mining service and the company is more focused on providing a wide range of trading options to users. Meanwhile, Binance strives to offer a wide range of cryptocurrency services globally.

OKX was released in spring 2017 and emerged as an offshoot of the original OKCoin platform (operating since 2013 in China). OKCoin now focuses on fiat currency exchange with cryptocurrencies, while OKX exchange focuses on cryptocurrency trading with a built-in API for algorithmic trading. The exchange also provides users with access to a multi-currency wallet and the ability for margin trading.

Founders are Jay Hao and Mingxing "Star" Xu. Jay Hao joined OKEx as CEO from the beginning and continues to hold the position. He has dedicated his career to technology and engineering. He has been following the blockchain industry for quite some time, with a focus on blockchain-based applications for video streaming and mobile gaming. Mingxing "Star" Xu founded OKCoin in China in 2013, and has since gained a great reputation in the industry. Today Xu is the CEO of OK Group.

Platform members can receive passive income if they have OKB in OKX Earn. Another purpose of the OKB token is to allocate funds to the OKEx Jumpstart platform. Participation in Jumpstart is only available after registering on the site.

OKB is used in the chain to facilitate spot trading, derivatives trading, and the simultaneous deployment of multiple scalable applications. In addition, a layered architecture reduces consensus times, improves scalability, and enhances security.

To add value to OKB and make the digital currency more attractive to holders, OKX burns OKB tokens every three months and records the burning of the coin on the official website. OKX uses 30% of commission revenue for this process. In addition, welcome bonuses are provided to new users.

The OKB token is similar to the Binance Coin (BNB). 50% of the service fee revenue is distributed among the token holders in proportion to their OKB balance. The benefits of the OKB token include: the right to vote on the platform, the ability to invest, and the ability to trade on OK.

There are 1 billion OKB tokens on the market with the following allocations: 40% to Founders, 10% to investors, 50% to AirDrop & Rewards, and 700 million OKBs are locked in until 2022.

Scan the QR code to sign in to the OKX exchange.

Binance Exchange

Binance is the world's largest exchange in terms of daily cryptocurrency trading volume. It is such a large exchange and with such good quality in all areas that we would say it is to cryptocurrencies what Amazon is to e-commerce.

Binance was founded in 2017 in China and is now registered in the Cayman Islands. It was founded by Changpeng Zhao, aka CZ, a developer who sold everything, went "All-in" on cryptocurrencies, and is now one of the richest and most powerful people in the world. Binance was originally headquartered in

China, but later moved its headquarters outside of China after the Chinese government's increasing regulatory interference with cryptocurrencies.

In 2019, Binance was banned in the United States for regulatory reasons. In response, Binance and other investors opened Binance.US, a separate exchange registered with the United States Financial Crimes Enforcement Network and designed to comply with all applicable USA laws.

In 2021, Binance came under investigation by both the United States Department of Justice and the Internal Revenue Service (IRS) following allegations of money laundering and tax violations. The UK Financial Conduct Authority ordered Binance to cease all regulated activity in the UK in June 2021.

Despite these actions, it continues to grow and constantly finds solutions to be in compliance with regulatory authorities. It is always willing to handle any problem and also help the regulators to do their job in this area. Although these may sound like bad facts, they are actually good because the cryptocurrency space is new and such actions are expected. Since it has overcome these issues without any serious problems so far, it means that it is just several steps ahead of any other platform in this field.

In 2005, CEO Changpeng Zhao founded Fusion Systems in Shanghai. The company built high-frequency trading systems for brokers. In 2013, he joined Blockchain.info as the third member of the cryptocurrency wallet team. He also worked briefly as CTO at OKCoin, a platform for spot trading between fiat and digital assets.

The Binance platform really offers everything! It has everything you can imagine about cryptocurrency finance and trading. Whatever is new and good will come out; whatever service around investment already has it or will put it up as soon as it is legally available. It really does it all!

Very important is the fact that they have very good customer service. If something happens to you and you lose your cryptocurrency… It goes without saying that they will take care of you, and they will take care of you in a quality way. The level of service that they have is equivalent to Amazon if you lose the product that you bought.

All this and more makes it the best and most secure cryptocurrency platform and application. It is my number 1 choice for both beginners and professionals.

Some Important Events

In January 2018, it was the largest cryptocurrency exchange with a market capitalization of $1.3 billion, a title it retained despite competition from Coinbase, among others.

In August 2018, Binance along with three other major exchanges raised $32 million for a stablecoin project. The idea of a stablecoin is to provide a cryptocurrency without the notorious volatility of Bitcoin and other popular digital assets.

In January 2019, Binance announced that it had partnered with Israel-based payment processor Simplex to enable cryptocurrency purchases with debit and credit cards, including Visa and Mastercard.

Cryptocurrencies of Binance

Binance Coin (BNB)

BNB was first launched through an initial coin offering (ICO) in 2017. Initially, it was issued as an ERC-20 digital token element on the Ethereum network, with a total supply limited to 200 million coins, of which 100 million BNB tokens were offered in the ICO. Shortly afterwards, Binance created its own network and moved all the tokens there. In April 2019, with the launch of the Binance Chain mainnet, ERC-20 BNB coins were exchanged for BEP2 BNB at a 1:1 ratio, which is much cheaper than ERC-20. After that, too many large projects were created on their own network.

BNB can be used as a payment method, as an auxiliary token for paying fees on Binance, and for participating in token sales on the Binance launchpad. BNB also powers the Binance DEX (Binance's decentralized exchange).

You can't mine BNB like you would a cryptocurrency like Bitcoin. Instead, there are validators that earn by validating blocks, thus maintaining network security. Of course, within the platform, there are many options to earn BNB simply by holding and using BNB. This is important, as it is the largest exchange in the world, with the highest trading volumes, which means that this currency is used to its fullest.

Binance regularly performs token burns on its currency, with the aim of reducing the total amount of BNB available on the market to 100 million tokens. This will help reduce supply and significantly increase the value of the currency.

Binance USD (BUSD)

Binance USD (BUSD) is a stable currency with 1:1 support to USD issued by Binance (in partnership with Paxos). It is approved and regulated by the New York State Department of Financial Services (NYDFS). The BUSD Monthly Audit Report is available on the official website. This project was launched on September 5, 2019 with the goal of combining dollar stability with blockchain technology. It is a way to provide security to individuals who want to use blockchain technology without fear of losing all their money overnight if the value of Bitcoin happens to drop.

Based on price stability, a stable currency plays an important role in transactions, payments, settlement, and Decentralized Financing (DeFi). It helps to perform many functions without changing the price either up or down.

Some general data about Binance

In general it is a very easy and secure platform. It's very professional but also very easy for a beginner. Anything new in the cryptocurrency market that is largely ethical, you can find it on Binance. It really offers you everything. But let's see what "everything" means.

Binance Academy

It provides full education about cryptocurrencies and everything around this field. And the best part? It's free! You can learn a lot and attend courses about cryptocurrencies. Not only do you not have to pay, but in many cases you earn money as a reward for completing one of their courses!

Binance Charity

An interesting part of Binance is also the social giving part, which they are very active in. They advertise it a lot to their audience. As a result, they have given millions of dollars of help in cases where it was needed. You can participate in donations related to major events happening around the world, such as the war in Ukraine. Of course, donations are made in cryptocurrencies.

Binance Card

This is where the dream becomes reality. Buy whatever you want with your cryptocurrency using your Binance card. The Binance card is a physical card that can be used to make purchases with your cryptocurrency anywhere that accepts Visa cards. So you can buy anywhere you would make purchases with another Visa card. You buy without having to do anything with your cryptocurrency. For example, if you have 100 dollars' worth of Bitcoin in your card, you just make the purchase and the card does the conversion automatically. You can also withdraw money from any ATM for a relatively small, extra fee (usually 2 to 4 dollars per transaction).

For card purchases, Binance charges almost nothing for transactions and also offers up to 8% cash back in BNB every time a purchase is made.

All funds are SAFU, meaning all funds and transactions on the Binance card are protected by Binance's world-class security.

It is also a very beautiful card!

Binance gift card

Like any big business, Binance has its own digital gift card that can be created in minutes and sent to a friend, relative, or anyone else as a gift to make purchases.

Binance Pay

Binance Pay is a contactless, borderless, and totally secure cryptocurrency payment technology designed by Binance. You can shop with cryptocurrencies or send cryptocurrencies to friends and family around the world.

You can pay, send, and receive cryptocurrency with zero commissions. Some shops and businesses that support Binance Pay are Travala, CryptoRefills HotDeals, Yummy Rides, Rewards Bunny, CryptoMate, Exeno, ByteTopUP, Lost Relics, Smile Shop, Coingate, Komilfo, Amoreshop, Royalpass, Uminer, Uquid, and Bitrefill.

There will be more to come in the future as the world of cryptocurrencies grows.

Binance Labs (Binance Labs)

Binance Labs identifies, invests in, and empowers sustainable blockchain entrepreneurs, startups, and communities by providing funding to industry-specific projects that help the broader development of the blockchain ecosystem.

They are also committed to supporting fast-paced technical teams that are positively impacting the cryptocurrency space and building the decentralized web.

Binance Launchpad

Binance's Launchpad and Launchpool platforms provide assistance and advice to teams of new projects on how best to issue and release their tokens. They provide a full package of services, starting with pre-token advisory services and continuing with post-marketing support and marketing. The goal is to enable these teams to focus on developing their project and continue to build products while handling marketing, exposure, and initial user base.

These platforms have already created some of the best encryption projects to date. If someone has a good idea, it's worth starting there because it is certain that Binance itself will sooner or later invest in their project. Of course, the very idea that a good project can get on the Binance platform is a great feat in itself and something that many companies have in their main goals to be able to expand.

Binance NFT Marketplace

Binance's NFT Marketplace attracts artists, creators, and crypto enthusiasts to create and exchange NFTs at much lower fees than a network like Ethereum. The platform currently has at least 3 product lines:

- Events where you can buy premium and exclusive NFTs created by top artists.
- The NFT Marketplace, where you can mint, buy, and submit offers for NFTs from creators around the world.
- Mystery Boxes, where you may have the chance to win rare NFTs from a box full of surprises.

The Binance exchange really has it all. The ones I mention above are some of the most important ones. Of course, the most basic use of Binance is as a cryptocurrency exchange and wallet. It has over 600 top cryptocurrencies at the time of this writing, and more are being added all the time. Every project has a dream of one day getting on its platform. It has staking options where you can make money just by "lending" them your money, but with great returns that are nothing like banking. It also provides great security in terms of not losing your cryptocurrencies, but it does not guarantee that you will definitely make a profit on your investment.

It has hundreds of other options with which you can make money just by applying them. You could really just have the Binance app on your mobile and, without doing anything else, you would have brought the whole world of cryptocurrency into your own world. We're talking about such a great company. If you just have Binance and Coinmarketcap (which is also owned by Binance) on your mobile, that's all you need in order to know everything about cryptocurrencies and be able to do almost anything. This applies to both beginners and professionals in the field.

Scan the QR code to sign in to the Binance exchange.

Bybit Exchange

Bybit, founded in March 2018, is one of the fastest growing cryptocurrency exchanges, with more than 5 million registered users by mid-2022. It's easy and comfortable to use, has many options and many cryptocurrencies, and is generally secure, with no major problems. The team behind it is constantly working to make it a powerful exchange.

This exchange looks like it follows Binance, and that's a good thing. It also gives its users many opportunities to earn money or coins. So it is very good for someone who can't invest a lot in cryptocurrencies, because through the app they will earn several cryptocurrencies that can be of great value in the years to come.

It also has options for staking and buying NFTs. It has very good customer support and, generally, the project is moving along quite well. So far, it has achieved everything it was supposed to without any problems, which indicates a good future for it. It has no problems with the network, nor with hacking, and especially with its liquidity.

As an exchange, it has its own currency, we would say, but that's not exactly the case. It has a large amount of BitDAO (BIT). BitDAO is a decentralized autonomous organization and has the cryptocurrency BIT. This protocol is one of the newest and largest decentralized autonomous organizations in the world that focuses on DeFi and is managed by BIT token holders.

Bybit's relationship with BitDAO is special, since BitDAO has no official founders. The project is maintained by a group of individuals who have contributed and own BIT tokens.

The protocol has no groups or companies behind it – as it is a DAO – which means that different people can propose changes to the BitDAO protocol. It is up to BIT holders (contributors) to vote on whether to accept or reject the proposals.

Bybit is an early supporter of BitDAO and has pledged to make recurring contributions to the BitDAO fund, which, at 2021 exchange rates, exceed $1 billion per year.

Bybit has the highest percentage of available BIT tokens, which is 60% at the time of project creation. These Bybit tokens can be used for research and development purposes.

One of the primary objectives of the initiative is to attract developers who have a talent for it. BitDAO's vision is open finance and a decentralized economy. BitDAO hopes to support a wide range of projects, including DeFi, DAOs, NFTs, and gaming. The support will be in the form of research and development, launchpool, and funding.

The BIT token has a maximum available quantity of 10,000,000,000 coins. The Bybit exchange has the largest percentage of it and uses it as if it were its own currency, we would say. It's a nice way for two different projects to work together.

Scan the QR code to sign in to the Bybit exchange.

Bitget Exchange

Have you heard about Bitget, the cryptocurrency exchange based in Seychelles? With a staggering 20 million users spanning 100 countries, Bitget is redefining the landscape of digital assets with its innovative features and an impressive lineup of partners.

Bitget's core focus revolves around copy trading and a suite of smart trading tools designed to empower both novice and experienced traders. Here's a glimpse of what they offer:

Diverse Crypto Services:

Bitget provides a wide range of crypto-related services. Whether you're into crypto-to-crypto trading, spot trading, futures trading, margin trading, or copy trading, Bitget has you covered. They even offer AI-powered trading bots for those looking to automate their strategies.

Token Launchpad:

Bitget's Launchpad is a springboard for promising projects, granting early access to high-quality tokens. As a Bitget Token (BGB) holder, you get to participate in voting for project listings, giving you a say in the platform's future.

Earning Services:

Bitget goes beyond trading with options for savings, staking, and even crypto loans. It's a holistic ecosystem designed to help you grow your crypto assets.

Star-Studded Partnerships:

Bitget proudly associates with renowned names like Lionel Messi, Adam DeVine, Juventus Football Club, PGL, Team Spirit, and DOTA 2 Bali Major. These partnerships signify Bitget's commitment to excellence and innovation.

Bitget Wallet:

But that's not all. Bitget Wallet, formerly known as Bitkeep, is a decentralized multi-chain wallet that combines wallets, swap transactions, NFTs, DApp markets, and Launchpad access. Supporting over 90 main chains, including ETH, BSC, Polygon, and Avalanche, it's all about versatility and convenience.

Bitget Token (BGB):

Bitget Token (BGB) is your ticket to an exclusive world of privileges and rights. With BGB in your wallet, you enjoy fee discounts, access to premium tokens via the Launchpad, and the power to influence project listings. There are 1.4 billion BGB coins in circulation, ensuring a thriving community experience.

In July 2023, Bitget unveiled a brand refresh, reinforcing its commitment to intelligent crypto trading with the motto "Trade smarter." This move solidified Bitget's standing as an industry leader, ready to shape the future of digital finance.

Meet the Visionaries:

Behind Bitget is a visionary team of early blockchain adopters, spearheaded by CEO Sandra Lou and Managing Director Gracy Chen. Their journey from traditional finance to blockchain technology in 2015 paved the way for Bitget's official launch in 2018.

Global Expansion:

Registered in Seychelles, Bitget operates in a decentralized manner but has ambitious plans to establish ideal headquarters. They've already set up regional hubs in Asia and LATAM markets and have their sights on expanding further into Europe and Africa.

For Everyone, Except a Few:

While Bitget serves customers in over 100 countries, there are a few exceptions. Due to regulations, they can't offer their products and services in countries like the US, Singapore, North Korea, Sudan, and others.

Your Crypto Playground:

With support for over 500 listed crypto tokens and more than 500 spot trading pairs, Bitget is the ultimate playground for crypto enthusiasts. From the classics like BTC and ETH to intriguing newcomers like BGB, PEPE, and SHIB, the possibilities are endless.

KuCoin Exchange

KuCoin is a Singapore-based cryptocurrency exchange. It was launched as an exchange on September 15, 2017. The company was founded in 2013 by the following individuals: Eric Don, Chief Operating Officer (COO), Jack Zhu, Director of Marketing, John Lee, President of Business Operations, Kent Li, Director of Operations and Maintenance, Linda Lin, Chief Legal Counsel, Michael Gan, Managing Director, and Top Lan, Chief Technical Officer (CTO).

The application is very easy, fast and secure. It has a lot of new quality projects, which are expected to go up a lot in the coming time once they are on the KuCoin platform. It is easy to use and without many complexities, so a beginner can use it to start his or her first investments.

KuCoin Token (KCS)

KCS is the native token of KuCoin. It was released in 2017 as a profit-sharing token that allows traders to derive value from trading. It was issued as an ERC-20 token, which runs on the Ethereum network and is supported by most Ethereum wallets. The total supply of KCS was set at 200 million tokens. There is a planned buyback and burn until there are only 100 million KCS tokens left. Sooner or later, when the KuCoin decentralized trading solution is released, KCS will be the native asset of KuCoin's decentralized financial services, as well as the KuCoin community governance token.

KuCoin also announced that "Empowering the KCS" will be a key priority for KuCoin. This will establish KCS as a strong product rather than a mere token, which will certainly further diversify the benefits that KCS holders can access.

In the long term, KCS will act as the key to the entire KuCoin ecosystem. With the development of DEX and KuChain, KCS will also be the key fuel and generic feature for future decentralized KuCoin products.

KCS Bonus is considered one of the best ways to earn passive income. Users who own more than 6 KCS tokens can receive a daily dividend, which is derived from 50% of the revenue from KuCoin's daily trading commission. KCS Bonus is a unique incentive mechanism for KCS holders and KuCoin ecosystem builders. The amount of rewards users can receive depends on the number of KCS tokens they own and the trading volume of the KuCoin exchange.

In addition to payment as a dividend, KCS, as a utility token, is also used to pay commissions for transactions made on the KuCoin exchange, allowing users to enjoy discounts on transaction commissions of up to 80%. KCS holders can become KuCoin VIPs, and users no longer need to have a huge volume of BTC transactions to unlock the reduced creator and recipient fees. KCS can also be used as a payment method for shopping, hotel reservations, purchasing gaming equipment, and more.

The initial KCS offering was set at 200 million tokens. KuCoin and the KCS team buy back KCS tokens from the market and burn them every quarter. The amount of KCS tokens burned depends on the quarterly trading volume on the KuCoin exchange. As a result, the circulating supply of KCS is reduced, and will eventually build up to 100 million tokens.

The KuCoin (KCS) token circulation is 80,118,638 KCS as of February 2021, with a maximum supply of 170,118,638 KCS.

KuCoin is another favorite multi-purpose exchange. It's just the thing for a newcomer to cryptocurrencies, but also for an old-timer who wants to do some transactions and trading quickly, without a lot of expenses and without doing much to get started, such as complex and time-consuming procedures like KYC (Know Your Customer). It is also a very secure platform and quite a big name in the cryptocurrency space.

Scan the QR code to sign in to the KuCoin exchange.

Gate.io Exchange

Gate.io was founded in 2013 and is also one of the largest and most secure exchanges. In terms of trading volume, Gate.io is one of the top 10 cryptocurrency exchanges in the world, with good quality cryptocurrency projects and a high rate of return. It is better known and more useful as a project that is new, but not that well known yet.

It's one of the platforms that uploads a lot of new cryptocurrencies, which can go up in value a lot, but of course they can also crash. In general, it uploads good projects and has a good security system. It's a good platform to open an account to see and buy a lot of new projects that can go up a lot in the future.

The platform has over 10 million users. It has its own blockchain, Gatechain, and is working on innovative products in cryptocurrencies. It offers almost all the options one needs in the cryptocurrency space.

Due to its many years of operation, it has proven its worth as a project. It has a lot of security, which sometimes gets tedious and makes the platform a bit more difficult for a new user, and that's its downside. Another disadvantage is that it charges a lot of transaction fees compared to other platforms, like Binance, for example.

Of course, Gate.io also has its own currency, which is the GT token. GT is the native token of the Gatechain mainnet. It officially became Gate.io's trading token on March 2, 2020 under the name GateToken. Since then, GT has been developed alongside Gate.io.

In its initial stage, GT was distributed to Gate.io Point buyers for free, as a gift, with an initial supply of 1 billion tokens. Subsequently, 0.7 billion of these were burned. The current total supply of the coin is 300 million tokens.

As an important part of the Gate.io ecosystem, the GT token can be used for scaling VIP tiers, transaction commission fees, participation in exclusive activities, and much more. Gate.io will also increasingly empower GT with more applications and options to improve its intrinsic value.

It's one of the bigger projects and it's going quite well, so it looks like the currency will follow that path. It has enough audience and almost all the options that a platform like this should have. Its focus is to upload new projects that aren't yet on other major platforms. In this way they attract a more specific audience to the platform, people who are willing to risk enough money to get a project that will make them rich.

Scan the QR code to sign in to the Gate exchange.

Platforms for Staking and Farming

Platforms to Earn Interest with Your Cryptocurrency

Now that we've covered the basics of cryptocurrencies, I'll give you a few facts about the main platforms I use to make more money just by holding my coins on them.

But what does it mean to make more money?

This means that you put your cryptocurrency on a platform, lock it up (usually, but not always) for a period of time, and earn a percentage of the money you put in. These are the so-called Farming and Staking pools, where you put your cryptocurrencies and lock them in for a period of time depending on the available offer. Then, you simply earn money according to the prices given by the platform, usually daily or weekly.

Below, I will give you the most reliable exchanges that give this option and have the highest returns.

Here is one last fact that is important before we start this analysis. If someone is afraid to invest in various cryptocurrencies because their prices can drop too low, these platforms also have options with stablecoins. Right now their return ranges from 5% to a little over 13% per year, and the risk is non-existent because the price of the coins is stable. It's like lending money to your bank, but here you earn a good interest rate.

If someone had 100,000 dollars to invest in something like this, like NEXO for example, which currently gives a 12% interest rate on stablecoins, they would make 12,000 dollars a year without doing anything and without changing the price of their investment. In other words, he doesn't care if the price of Bitcoin goes up or down. But he would care if he had put the 100,000 dollars in Bitcoin on another platform with an interest rate of 40%. Bitcoin can go up, but it can also go down. So, at the end of the year, he may end up with less, because quite simply the price of Bitcoin has halved.

Of course, this is just one example I give you to show how amazing this new economy is, where you can make so much with zero risk. If you go to a bank, you won't even make 3%.

I personally invest in cryptocurrencies because I believe that they will inevitably increase in value in the future, while at the same time enjoying higher rates of return on my investment.

But there is always the risk that the company, institution, or organization you have invested your money in will go out of business. Also, on a planet like ours, one can never be absolutely sure, especially with the "crazy" manipulation that exists in the markets. But the following platforms are the ones that have the highest security in the market and, really, if something happened to them, it would have a very big impact on the entire cryptocurrency market. However, for your peace of mind, these platforms are secured in a number of ways so that you can get your money back if something happens to them.

So, let's see them.

OKX

The OKX platform provides users with various ways to earn cryptocurrency. OKX Earn currently offers eight products with which one can earn by allocating their cryptocurrency.

Dual Investment

Dual Investment is an OKX Earn product that allows users to generate an attractive return on the assets they own. Currently, it supports investments in BTC, ETH, and USDT.

Dual Investment is an unprotected investment product, which means that the capital you initially invest is at risk. However, the product provides a predictable return on an investment regardless of the direction of future price movement.

Saving

The "Saving" product enables OKX platform users to earn interest by depositing their digital assets on the platform. The deposited assets are lent to traders as margin loans and OKX then collects and distributes interest to users. Interest is collected on an hourly basis and the terms are flexible – meaning you can withdraw your assets within an hour of request.

Staking

Some cryptocurrencies use the Proof of Staking mechanism. The process of staking is quite complicated and is not recommended for novice users. OKX's staking products take care of the technical details on your behalf, greatly simplifying the process. With just a few clicks, you can contribute your assets to support your favorite Proof of Staking networks.

DeFi

OKX took the initiative to add several DeFi products to the Earn section to make it easier for users, and lower the barriers to entry for those seeking passive income opportunities in this growing niche.

DOT and KSM slot auctions

The Polkadot network includes a main relay chain connected to numerous parachains. Because the number of possible parachains is limited, voting determines which candidate will receive what is known as a parachain slot. Anyone can participate in the voting process using DOT or KSM, and often receives rewards in the project's native tokens for doing so. The same process applies to Polkadot's "canary network," Kusama.

Staking ETH 2.0

Ethereum staking is already available and you can participate through the OKX platform. Here, staking in ETH is a user-friendly alternative with a flexible exit policy and a much lower entry barrier.

Jumpstart

Users of the OKX platform can also generate passive income by providing liquidity to cryptocurrency projects launched through their incubator, OKX Jumpstart.

P2P lending

OKX's P2P lending product also provides an opportunity for users to generate passive income with their cryptocurrency. Users can lend their assets to borrowers on the platform and earn interest on the borrowed funds.

Scan the QR code to sign in to OKX.

Binance

It goes without saying that the "Amazon" of cryptocurrencies could not be missing here. The platform features almost all the top cryptocurrencies. It provides much better rates than platforms that have their own tokens because it has the power to do so due to its audience size.

We talked a lot about Binance earlier in the book. Some key facts are that here you will find almost all cryptocurrencies available for staking, usually every 30, 60, 90, or 120 days. That means you lock them in for that many days and you get paid every day for all of those days, according to the rate it gives you.

So you can only put in simple cryptocurrencies, which can go up or down in price, unlike stablecoin which is stable.

Security?

I don't need to say anything here. If something happens to Binance, it will have such a huge impact on the entire cryptocurrency world that it won't even make sense how much security any other project or platform has, like Nexo for example. Everything will collapse. So, there's no point in getting into this, since it's the biggest cryptocurrency exchange project and it's going up all the time.

It goes without saying that it has a good protection system based on its own currency, and very good customer service that will help anyone with any problem they encounter.

I don't need to say much here, as you will find everything very easily on their platform. I have already written a lot about Binance. By the way, one could write a whole book just about Binance.

At this point I will add a relatively new platform to make money. It is backed by Binance and is in almost every category the best of all the projects that Binance supports. In addition to Binance's support, it is the first platform with an official partnership and backup support on the topic of staking from Binance itself. That platform is Biswap.

Bybit

Bybit is a well-established cryptocurrency exchange known for its diverse offerings, including crypto derivatives, spot trading, and a range of other products. While it primarily serves as a trading platform, it also provides opportunities for users to explore staking and farming options within the crypto ecosystem.

Staking: Bybit allows users to stake certain cryptocurrencies in return for rewards. Staking involves locking up your tokens in a wallet to support the network's operations and, in turn, earning staking rewards. Bybit provides staking services for a selection of tokens, and users can participate to earn rewards based on the specific terms of each staking program.

Farming: Bybit offers opportunities for users to participate in liquidity provision, earning rewards in the form of tokens or additional assets for their contributions to the platform's liquidity ecosystem.

It's important to note that the specific cryptocurrencies available for staking and farming, as well as the terms and rewards associated with these programs, may change over time. Users interested in staking or farming on Bybit should regularly check the platform for the latest information on available opportunities.

Bitget

Bitget is a cryptocurrency exchange based in Seychelles, offering a wide range of services to over 20 million users across 100 countries. While Bitget primarily focuses on trading, it also provides opportunities for staking and farming within the cryptocurrency ecosystem.

Bitget offers users the ability to participate in staking programs and in liquidity provision, enabling them to earn additional tokens or assets as rewards for contributing to the platform's liquidity ecosystem.in liquidity provision, enabling them to earn additional tokens or assets as rewards for contributing to the platform's liquidity ecosystem.

The details of available staking and farming programs, including supported cryptocurrencies and associated rewards, may vary and should be checked on the platform.

Nexo

Here you have opportunities to earn up to 16% APR (Annual Percentage Rate), paid daily with compound interests, flexible earnings, and zero fees.

Buying cryptocurrencies and HODL (hold cryptocurrencies for a long time with the aim of increasing the value over time – investing for a long time) until the price goes up is an excellent option for making a profit. It does require a lot of time and a lot of luck with Nexo, but it is an opportunity to immediately put your dormant assets to work and have a predictable source of passive income.

Registering on the Nexo platform takes less than a minute. With some basic knowledge, you can go through most of the steps very easily, until you make your money have a good return.

Open the Nexo platform or the Nexo app, complete the verification, buy or transfer cryptocurrencies to your account, and you're done. Simply tap the Earn option to have your cryptocurrencies earn interest daily.

Nexo is raising the bar for the entire blockchain space by using the most stringent KYC (Know Your Customer) and AML (Anti Money Laundering) policies. It also employs impeccable risk assessment, data protection, and enhanced cyber security.

Some data from the company itself about its high security:

- 256-bit military-grade encryption for every account in Nexo.
- Storage in Class III vaults through leading blockchain custodians including BitGo, Ledger Vault, and others.
- $375 million of insurance from their custodian partners through Lloyd's of London and Marsh & Arch.
- The ISO/IEC 27001:2013 certificate, which guarantees Nexo's security infrastructure, is of a high standard.
- 200-500% super secure encryption credit lines. Nexo never issues credit on an unsecured basis, ensuring our funds are backed regardless of how the market moves.

Nexo currently serves more than five million users in more than 200 jurisdictions and manages more than $4 billion in assets. The company employs about 150 people at the time of writing, with its management based in London.

Nexo was founded by a group of financial professionals and cryptocurrency enthusiasts who turned to the blockchain to create a cryptocurrency equivalent to a service well-established in traditional finance but non-existent in digital. This service is lending against the value of one's assets while retaining ownership of them. In 2018, the team launched the Nexo platform, offering the world's first cryptocurrency credit lines. They allowed digital asset holders to receive fiat and stablecoin loans against their cryptocurrencies, laying the foundation for cryptocurrency lending.

Nexo is marketed to individual and institutional investors, cryptocurrency companies, exchanges, miners, and others who want liquidity from their assets. The company earns from interest accrued on loans. It also offers institutional lending and advisory services.

Nexo has its own token. It distributes 30% of its profits to NEXO token holders in the form of dividends.

Nexo has a fixed supply of 1 billion NEXO tokens.

It's another favorite platform, and I use it often. Of course, I can't guarantee that it will be functional forever. Right now, as I'm writing the book, another platform, Celsius Network, with a similar product to Nexo's, has failed. It was a platform that seemed to be doing well, and I wanted to include it in this book. But after liquidity problems in the markets in the first half of 2022, Celsius Network didn't make it.

The same could happen to Nexo at some point, although that platform seems to be much more ready to face such a test. Either way, these platforms have their risks. One should study them and keep up to date with the cryptocurrency market all the time, because there is no telling what will happen in the future. As there are not enough controls by governments, a lot can happen.

Scan the QR code to register with Nexo.

PancakeSwap

PancakeSwap is a decentralized exchange based on the Binance Smart Chain. It was released by an anonymous team of developers.

The PancakeSwap logo represents a pancake. The Pancake cryptocurrency has been compared to SushiSwap in the past. However, ShushiSwap is built on top of the Ethereum blockchain, which can be much more expensive, while PancakeSwap is based on the Binance Smart Chain, which is much cheaper to trade.

The platform was released in September 2020. While we don't really know who the development team behind the platform is, it has been regularly audited by blockchain security companies like Slowmist and Certik. It has frequent security checks so you can exchange PancakeSwap's CAKE and other assets with peace of mind.

PancakeSwap has community governance. It gives users the ability to farm, provides tokens, and incorporates other specific features that make it stand out and allow you to earn percentages on your investments.

PancakeSwap has its own cryptocurrency, CAKE, with a maximum supply of 750 million coins.

UniSwap

Uniswap is an automated cryptocurrency exchange based on Ethereum. It has its own native token, UNI, which is known as a governance token.

Uniswap is also completely open source, which means that anyone can copy the code to create their own decentralized exchanges. According to the latest data, Uniswap is currently in the top 5 largest DeFi projects.

The UNI token was originally created in September 2020 in an attempt to prevent users from defecting to the rival DEX SushiSwap. A month before the UNI tokens were released, SushiSwap, a fork of Uniswap, urged Uniswap users to allow SushiSwap to reallocate their money to the new platform by rewarding them with SUSHI. This was a new type of token that gave users governance rights over the new protocol, as well as a proportional amount of all transaction fees paid to the platform.

Uniswap responded by creating 1 billion UNI tokens and decided to distribute 150 million of them to anyone who had ever used the platform. Each person received 400 UNI. Thus, the platform's maximum UNI offer is set at 1 billion UNI tokens.

5 AI Cryptocurrency Projects

Worldcoin (WLD)

Worldcoin is a project with a mission to create the world's largest identity and financial network, designed to be a public utility that is accessible to everyone. At its core, the Worldcoin system revolves around a concept known as "World ID," a privacy-focused global identity network. Here's a breakdown of the key features and components of the Worldcoin project:

World ID – A Privacy-Preserving Identity Network:

World ID is designed to enable users to verify their identity online while maintaining their privacy through the use of zero-knowledge proofs. It introduces the concept of "Proof of Personhood" as a means of confirming one's humanness in an online context.

To participate in the Worldcoin ecosystem, individuals are required to download the "World App," which serves as the first wallet app supporting the creation of a World ID. To get their World ID "Orb-verified," individuals visit a physical imaging device called an "Orb."

Orbs are typically operated by a network of independent local businesses known as "Orb Operators." These Orbs use multispectral sensors to verify the user's humanness and uniqueness. Importantly, all images captured during the verification process are promptly deleted on the device by default, with user consent required for any data storage.

WLD Tokens and Governance:

All Orb-verified World ID holders are entitled to claim recurring grants of free WLD tokens. Notably, these tokens are not available in the United States. The WLD token is designed as a utility token with governance properties.

Users holding WLD tokens have a say in the future of the protocol, and the governance model introduces the possibility of "one-person-one-vote" mechanisms alongside the traditional "one-token-one-vote" system. The community and Worldcoin Foundation will collaborate on how World ID and the WLD token interact within the governance model.

Beyond governance, WLD tokens may serve various purposes, such as facilitating actions within the World App, making payments, or signaling approval for specific initiatives or causes.

WLD is an ERC-20 token based on the Ethereum blockchain. Users receive their user grants on the Optimism Mainnet, making most WLD transactions likely to occur on the Optimism network.

The initial total supply of WLD tokens is 10 billion. For the first 15 years following launch, this supply is capped at 10 billion, enforced by the WLD smart contract. After this period, governance may introduce an inflation rate of up to 1.5% per year if deemed necessary for the protocol's long-term sustainability.

The allocation of the 10 billion WLD tokens is distributed among various stakeholders, with 75% designated for the Worldcoin community, 9.8% for the Initial Development Team, 13.5% for TFH Investors, and 1.7% for the TFH Reserve.

What Sets Worldcoin Apart:

Worldcoin's uniqueness lies in its ambition to create a global identity and financial network accessible to a billion people. In contrast to many other cryptocurrency projects, Worldcoin's primary focus is on distributing the majority of WLD tokens to individuals simply for being human.

World ID is at the core of this effort, allowing individuals to prove their unique human identity to various platforms, including social networks and government programs. This approach has the potential to enable fairer distribution of resources, protect against bots, and even support novel forms of governance.

Worldcoin has already made significant progress, with over two million people from more than 30 countries verifying their identity at Orbs during the pre-launch phase. As the project advances, Worldcoin plans to deploy 1,500 Orbs across multiple cities and countries to meet the growing demand for World ID.

Worldcoin's commitment to transparency and its unique approach to identity verification set it apart within the cryptocurrency space, as it strives to create a network with widespread global adoption.

The Graph (GRT)

We saw this project again on the top 20 projects but here am gonna just include some of its AI features and why it is included in the AI section.

The Graph Protocol, often referred to as an "AI token," plays a pivotal role as a critical infrastructure layer that enables the development of AI applications on top of blockchain data. While not inherently dependent on Artificial Intelligence, The Graph's significance in the AI landscape stems from its ability to simplify the process of accessing and extracting extensive blockchain data, a fundamental requirement for many AI applications.

It's important to note that The Graph isn't exclusively tailored for AI applications. Instead, it serves as a versatile tool that can be harnessed by developers for various decentralized applications (dApps), including but not limited to AI-related projects.

Developers working with dApps can configure their smart contracts to be understood by The Graph, allowing it to create what is known as a "subgraph." This concept is akin to websites generating index files to facilitate search engine accessibility, as exemplified by Google.

"Google of Blockchain" is The Graph's Nickname. The Graph has earned the moniker of the 'Google of Blockchain' due to its ability to swiftly and efficiently index and retrieve blockchain data. In a parallel to Google's use of advanced algorithms and machine learning to organize vast internet data, The Graph employs robust indexing algorithms to enable the rapid access of blockchain data. To put it succinctly, if Google is today's internet search engine, The Graph aspires to be the Web3 search engine of the future.

When it comes to developing decentralized applications on networks like Ethereum, access to data is a fundamental requirement, particularly on-chain data. While Ethereum offers extensive open data, the challenge lies in sifting through specific data to construct more intricate dApps. Indexing blockchain data can be a complex and arduous task for developers.

The Graph offers a solution to this issue through its technology, simplifying the process of retrieving both simple and complex data. This accessibility empowers developers to construct diverse and sophisticated dApps without the hurdles typically associated with managing blockchain data.

Fetch.ai (FET)

Fetch.ai, founded in 2017 and introduced through an IEO on Binance in March 2019, is an AI lab with a mission to create an open, decentralized machine learning network with a crypto economy. This project aims to democratize access to artificial intelligence technology by establishing a permissionless network where anyone can connect and access secure datasets. Fetch.ai leverages autonomous AI to execute tasks, drawing from its extensive global network of data. The project's model is deeply rooted in addressing use cases such as optimizing DeFi trading services, enhancing transportation networks (including parking and micromobility), refining smart energy grids, and revolutionizing travel, among other applications reliant on extensive datasets.

Fetch.ai was founded by Toby Simpson, Humayun Sheikh, and Thomas Hain. Humayun Sheikh currently serves as the CEO of Fetch.ai, bringing his extensive experience from other projects like Mettalex, uVue, and itzMe. Toby Simpson, formerly the COO of Fetch.ai, now sits on the Advisory Board, and he has a history of leadership roles at Ososim Limited and DeepMind. Thomas Hain, the former Chief Science Officer, was a co-founder and director of Koemei.

Unique Features of Fetch.ai:

Fetch.ai's utility token, FET, plays a pivotal role in the project by facilitating the creation, deployment, and training of digital twins. These digital twins are integral to smart contracts and oracles on the platform. Users can harness FET to construct and deploy their own digital twins on the network. Developers, by paying with FET tokens, can access machine-learning-based utilities to train autonomous digital twins and deploy collective intelligence across the network.

The validation nodes on Fetch.ai operate through staking FET tokens, serving to facilitate network validation and establish reputation. This mechanism enhances the platform's security and integrity.

The Fetch.ai technology stack comprises four distinctive elements:

Digital Twin Framework: This provides modular components to aid teams in building marketplaces, skills, and intelligence for digital twins to connect with.

Open Economic Framework: It delivers search and discovery functions for digital twins.

Digital Twin Metropolis: This involves a collection of smart contracts running on a WebAssembly (WASM) virtual machine to maintain an immutable record of agreements between digital twins.

Fetch.ai Blockchain: This combines multi-party cryptography and game theory to offer secure, censorship-resistant consensus. It supports rapid chain-syncing, vital for digital twin applications.

The core components of the platform include the learner, where each participant is an integral part of the learning process, representing a unique private dataset and machine learning system. The global market results from a collective learning experiment, with the machine learning model trained collaboratively by the participants. The Fetch.ai Blockchain supports smart contracts that enable coordination and governance in a secure and auditable manner. Lastly, the decentralized data layer, based on IPFS, enables the sharing of machine learning weights among all participants.

Token Supply:

As of February 2021, Fetch.ai (FET) boasts a circulating supply of 746,113,681 tokens, with a maximum supply capped at 1,152,997,575 FET. This finite supply underlines the token's scarcity and its role within the Fetch.ai ecosystem.

Ocean Protocol (OCEAN)

Ocean Protocol is a groundbreaking project that harnesses the synergy of blockchain technology, decentralized networks, and advanced cryptographic techniques to facilitate secure and privacy-conscious data sharing. Its primary objective is to lay the foundation for a new Data Economy that empowers data owners with control over their data while upholding privacy. This initiative also aims to catalyze the commercialization of data, including the creation of data marketplaces.

The minds behind Ocean Protocol possess a diverse and deep-rooted background in significant domains, including big data, blockchain, artificial intelligence, and data exchanges. They complement this expertise with real-world business experience as entrepreneurs, designers, and technologists. Additionally, Ocean Protocol benefits from the guidance of over 35 advisors worldwide, all of whom are renowned for their expertise in AI, blockchain, big data, business, and policy. These advisors have been carefully selected due to their shared commitment to unlocking the potential of data and AI for the betterment of society.

Unique Aspects of Ocean Protocol:

Ocean Protocol distinguishes itself by enabling access to data that was previously inaccessible or difficult to obtain. It achieves this by allowing individuals in possession of sought-after datasets to tokenize their data and list it on the Ocean Market. This not only creates an additional source of income for data publishers but also grants scientists, researchers, data analysts, and other stakeholders access to a more extensive and reliable data pool.

Furthermore, Ocean Protocol equips organizations with the tools to create and launch their data markets. This can be achieved either by directly forking the Ocean Protocol or by leveraging the Ocean Protocol React hooks provided. Comprehensive documentation is readily available to guide entities through this process.

Holders of OCEAN tokens have the opportunity to lock their tokens at df.oceandao.org and earn VeOcean. Subsequently, they can opt for passive rewards by retaining their VeOcean holdings or engage in active rewards by staking VeOcean and potentially offering datasets for sale, thus earning additional rewards.

Token Supply:

As of October 2023, the entire OCEAN token supply will have been minted, which is 1,410,000,000 OCEAN. The proceeds from this supply are placed into oceanDAO multisignature wallets that involve seven signees. These signees include core members of the Ocean team, Ocean community members, and founders of other web3 projects. Notably, the core team members represent a minority of the signees, ensuring a diverse and community-driven approach to managing the token supply.

SingularityNET (AGIX)

SingularityNET is an innovative blockchain-powered platform designed to facilitate the creation, sharing, and monetization of AI services on a global scale. Its central feature is an accessible AI marketplace where users can seamlessly explore, evaluate, and purchase a wide array of AI services using the platform's native utility token, AGIX. This marketplace also serves as a platform for AI developers to showcase and sell their AI tools while conveniently monitoring their performance.

The driving force behind SingularityNET is a team of visionaries who played a pivotal role in the development of Sophia, often referred to as the "world's most expressive robot." The core mission of SingularityNET is to empower Sophia to comprehend human language fully and to continue advancing "OpenCog," an AI framework with aspirations of achieving "advanced general intelligence," a level of artificial intelligence on par with or surpassing human capabilities.

SingularityNET was initially introduced in 2017 and successfully conducted an initial coin offering (ICO) in December of the same year, raising an astounding $36 million in just one minute.

Founders of SingularityNET:

The team at SingularityNET comprises a talented roster of AI scientists, developers, researchers, and engineers. The project was established by Dr. Ben Goertzel, who serves as SingularityNET's CEO and chief scientist, along with Simone Giacomelli and Dr. David Hanson.

Dr. Ben Goertzel is a prominent figure in the AI and robotics domain, with a distinguished track record of collaborating with cutting-edge technology companies, including Hanson Robotics and the OpenCog Foundation. He also holds the positions of chief scientist at Mozi Health and vice chairman for Humanity+.

Simone Giacomelli, an entrepreneur and investor, previously worked for crypto consultancy Cryptodex before shifting his focus to the technology R&D lab Vulpem, which he founded in 2015.

Dr. David Hanson, the third co-founder of SingularityNET, boasts a lengthy and diverse history in the robotics sector, having worked with Disney and founded several robotics startups, such as Human Emulation Robotics, Initiative for Awakening Machines, and Hanson Robotics.

Unique Aspects of SingularityNET:

SingularityNET stands out as the first platform that streamlines the process of AI tool and library sales for developers while providing buyers with the opportunity to test AI services from the marketplace before making a financial commitment. This unique feature ensures that customers can verify if an AI service aligns with their requirements.

Additionally, those seeking specific AI services can leverage SingularityNET's extensive community of AI experts through the Request for AI portal (RFAI). This portal enables customers to commission new AI tools, while developers can earn AGIX tokens by fulfilling these requests.

The utility of the AGIX token has continually evolved with the expansion of the SingularityNET ecosystem. Features like the SingularityNET Enhancement Proposal (SNEP) have enabled AGIX holders to vote on network operational changes. Staking was also introduced, allowing users to stake their tokens.

In collaboration with Hanson Robotics, SingularityNET has ventured into Awakening Health, a joint project dedicated to harnessing AI for healthcare applications. Their first product, Grace, is a humanoid assistant designed for the healthcare sector.

Token Circulation:

As of February 2021, approximately 861.5 million AGIX tokens, representing 86% of the total supply, were in circulation. The significant token supply reflects substantial dilution. Half (50%) of the total AGIX supply was distributed during SingularityNET's 2017 ICO. The remaining distribution includes 20% reserved for early developer and partner incentives, 18% for core team members, 8% allocated to the SingularityNET foundation for long-term platform development, and 4% set aside for security bounties.

The Future – Web 3.0/Web3

Imagine a new kind of internet that not only perfectly interprets what one enters, but also understands everything that is conveyed through text, voice, or any other medium. A place where all the content one consumes is much more tailored to him or her than ever before.

We are on the verge of a new phase of the Web revolution, which some pioneers and enthusiasts call Web 3.0 – the next generation of the Web after the first and current one.

In Web 3.0, data is connected in a decentralized way, enabling a huge leap into a future where we don't rely on centralized repositories to store data. In addition, machines and users will be able to communicate and interact with data in a more specialized and holistic way.

For this to happen, programs need to understand data and information both contextually and conceptually. Since Web 3.0 networks will operate through decentralized protocols – the fundamental blocks of cryptocurrency and blockchain technology – we can expect strong overlap between these technologies and other fields.

They will be essentially interoperable, fully integrated, and automated through smart contracts. They will be used to enable anything, even microtransactions in remote accessible areas.

In a world powered by blockchains, transparency will be the easiest thing. Companies will compete to be more transparent and substantially better than others, as more transparency brings in more investors and other participants.

Imagine a world where content creators earn directly from their audience, advertising agencies pay publishers directly for their ads, or a company's taxi drivers earn directly from their passengers! This is exactly the promise of a new world brought by Web 3.0! No middlemen, no lying in the middle, where anything of real value gets its real value.

Since the distributed ledger will allow shared access to everyone on the network, there will be transparency everywhere. All stakeholders will be constantly aware of the value and the product they are dealing with and will not rely on intermediaries to provide access to that data.

A blockchain, by definition, is an immutable distributed ledger that allows everyone to see every transaction. This technology can usher in a new era of financial transparency and achieve better behavior. Transparency is by far the best regulator, as it optimizes asset prices and exposes the quality of goods and services to the public.

Web 3.0 is built using the blockchain as a building block. Thus, it is innovating in various industries such as payment processing, property and land titles, intellectual property ownership and protection, digital identifiers, and, of course, cryptocurrencies.

Cryptocurrencies are not competing to replace traditional fiat currencies such as the dollar. They are an asset class and a utility in decentralized blockchain networks, which can be purchased using fiat currencies.

Web 3.0's intention is to operate through decentralized protocols, which are essential components of cryptocurrency and blockchain technology. This will cause an expanding relationship between these technologies.

Here are 10 more Web 3.0 cryptocurrencies beyond the known ones (Ethereum, BNB, Sol, ADA, Elrond) for 2022.

1. Helium (HNT)

Helium is a decentralized blockchain-powered network for Internet of Things (IoT) devices using the Proof of Coverage algorithm.

With Helium, users can create decentralized wireless infrastructure at any scale. They allow low-power devices to communicate with each other and transmit data over a network consisting of nodes called hotspots, each covering a specific portion of the network. Hotspots also serve as miners. Network users who purchase or create a hotspot also act as network nodes and mine HNT, which is the native cryptocurrency of the Helium network.

2. Chainlink (LINK)

Chainlink is a decentralized network based on Ethereum. It facilitates the creation of smart contracts based on real-world data. It can be integrated into any blockchain, which is why it has become a widely used platform for Oracle services.

Chainlink's native currency, LINK, has seen increased demand recently. At one point it surpassed Shiba Inu as the most-traded and owned cryptocurrency by the largest Ethereum holders.

3. Filecoin (FIL)

Filecoin is a decentralized peer-to-peer storage network, where users can earn the platform's token by renting space on their computer hard drives. One of Filecoin's main advantages is that it can store digital assets, such as art or music, behind NFTs.

Anyone can be a storage provider on the Filecoin network, whether an individual or a data center. All someone needs is internet access and enough disk space on their computer. The more storage space they provide on the Filecoin network, the more transaction and token fees they can earn.

4. Flux (FLUX)

Flux is designed to help developers create Web 3.0 applications and deploy them across different networks simultaneously. It can also be used to create decentralized projects. Flux offers an Oracle project with an exclusively decentralized infrastructure that allows users to access data on and off the chain.

5. Theta (THETA)

Theta is a decentralized blockchain network created specifically for video streaming. As a peer-to-peer network, Theta aims to facilitate video delivery for users, with enterprise validation nodes from Sony, Google, Samsung, and other companies.

6. The Graph (GRT)

The Graph is an indexing system that can be used to organize blockchain data. Members can filter index data and perform searches. It is also a low-level blockchain index creation protocol, as well as a high-level cryptographic ledger based on this protocol.

7. BitTorrent (BTT)

BitTorrent is a data transfer protocol over the internet. It offers a reliable solution for transferring very large files, such as audio or video files, turning each user's computer into a redistribution point.

With more than 2 billion users and 200 million wallets, BitTorrent is a leading peer-to-peer file sharing platform, featuring torrent software for Mac, Android, Windows, and more. Torrents are the most popular form of modern peer-to-peer file sharing. It is touted as "the world's largest distributed network" and provides secure streaming and downloading for torrent products.

8. Siacoin (SC)

Sia is a peer-to-peer digital platform where users can pay hosts to rent storage space in the cloud. User data is encrypted into 30 segments, each of which is uploaded to a different host.

Skynet, which does the programming for Sia, is preparing several new projects based on Sia, such as cloud media streaming, content delivery, and file sharing.

9. Basic Attention Token (BAT)

BAT powers a blockchain-based digital advertising platform that delivers content through the Brave browser. Advertisers pay for their ad campaigns using BAT. Part of the BAT they pay is distributed to users as a reward for viewing ads. Although the BAT environment protects user privacy, advertisers can target their ads to maximize their effectiveness.

10. Polkadot (DOT)

Polkadot allows the transfer of any asset or data to blockchain. Its service is not limited to tokens. Its users can interoperate with multiple blockchains on Polkadot's native network. What sets Polkadot apart from other competing networks, such as Ethereum, is that these chains, called "parachains," are unique and independent, but can communicate with each other – a vital function for Web 3.0.

Finally, considering the advent of Web 3.0, the rise of Web 3.0 cryptocurrencies is inevitable.

Web 3.0 is based on concepts of greater utility, transparency, and decentralization. As the number of supporters of these ideas grows daily, their greater support could result in Web 3.0 tokens becoming profitable investments. Overall, our future seems to be Web 3.0, so it would be good to have invested in companies that will be there in the future.

Decentralized Means of Social Networking

NFTs and Metaverse were the hottest topics in the cryptocurrency ecosystem in 2021, but the next big thing may be decentralized social media. Like decentralized finance, decentralized social media platforms have no centralized governing body. They may, one day, provide viable alternatives to established platforms like Twitter, Instagram, Facebook, and TikTok, especially after the many problems we've seen in recent years with censorship. The technology is currently evolving and is just above the embryonic stage of development.

Centralized social media platforms are unfair to community members and content creators. It's pretty obvious that centralized social networks are prone to a lot of shady stuff, with mysterious algorithms controlling what people see, and people getting banned for whatever reason. The centralized social media industry is plagued by global censorship, lack of customization, unfair revenue generation, algorithmic dictatorship, and a monopoly on network effects.

Decentralized social media is really about returning power to the citizens and the hot topic of free speech. Traditional social media platforms are completely autonomous and the host company controls the data servers. Twitter owns and controls all of its content, or in other words, all of your content. The same is the case with Instagram, Facebook, TikTok, etc.

So, a platform on a public blockchain is able to not only offer more security to our data, but also freedom of speech, without allowing any authority to maliciously interfere and censor. Of course, this can be bad in some cases, where some people will take advantage of this right, the "excessive" freedom of speech, but surely, it is better to be able to communicate than not to be able to express oneself on a topic.

So here is a collection of some well-known social blockchain network applications that help freedom of speech and more, as we will see below.

All.me

All.me is a multi-purpose cryptocurrency blockchain platform that features both social media and regular cryptocurrency exchange functions. It is one of the fastest blockchain communities and has millions of active users, exchanging cryptocurrencies, sharing opinions, and seamlessly improving the entire community. All.me has a similar user interface to Facebook, but it is not fully followed. Users can view posts, content, ads, etc., and earn reward points. One can either exchange real cash to get points or invest in cryptocurrencies. All.me allows users to add cryptocurrency wallets to their accounts and make transactions instantly. There are no fees in the registration process.

Mastodon.social

Mastodon.social is not only a simple social networking platform, but one of the most remarkable ones. That's right. It is the lightest and fastest social networking community for the western world. You obviously know about Discord, an extremely popular social platform in the world. Mastodon.social has almost similar user interface as Discord. The difference is that here there is full access to the blockchain network system through Mastodon.social. One can also buy and sell cryptocurrencies and do trading easily with the MT5 platform integration. This platform has anti-abuse tools to help you stay safe. You will receive a specific key that you need to enter when it comes to approving anything. So, even if someone has access to someone else's phone, they can't activate any event on their Mastodon.social account without that code.

Minds.com

Minds.com is a social networking application based on the blockchain system. It is a fully decentralized platform that has all the functions of social media, such as posting videos, blogs, images, and statuses. Direct messages and group messages can be sent from both the mobile app and the website. People around the world can connect with each other through *Minds.com*. Another great feature is that you can trade in cryptocurrencies (BTC, ETH, ZCash, etc.). In addition, by meeting certain criteria, you can earn tokens daily through contributions. These tokens can be redeemed for channel upgrades, promotion, content enhancement, and more.

Steemit

Steemit is very similar to Reddit and is one of the most advanced blockchain social networks in the world. Steemit is fast and has a lot to offer to users. There is something about it that makes it exceptional in the crowd. You can earn cryptocurrency on Steemit for everything you do. You can post any content and whenever you receive positive votes, you win. You can contribute to society by undoing the worst content and earn cryptocurrency as a reward. It's a double win situation. Steemit uses a completely new cryptocurrency system that differs from regular cryptocurrencies like BTC, ETH, etc. While regular cryptocurrencies are created through the computing power of miners, Steemit users themselves create cryptocurrencies with their activity in the community. So, you can say that Steemit is a social network for you, based on a blockchain community.

SocialX

SocialX is a community-driven social networking platform. You might find it very similar to Facebook or Instagram, but there's a big difference here. SocialX is a decentralized blockchain platform. Users can earn cryptocurrencies through rewards in SOCX tokens. Anything you do here, such as "like," comments, sharing, etc., will earn you reward points. Similarly, you will earn a lot of points by posting content regularly. Moreover, you can earn even more reward points by getting super likes from users.

DLive.tv

DLive.tv is one of the most popular social networking communities in the world. It is an online community very similar to Twitch.tv (a live video streaming service owned by Twitch Interactive, a subsidiary of Amazon). This platform only supports live streaming and makes profits through it. It is also a decentralized blockchain social networking website. It has its own cryptocurrency "Lemon" as a medium of exchange. You can post on your social profile live events, news, games, crafts and almost anything you want to earn Lemon. Just log on to DLive.tv and you'll see what it's all about.

Honest.cash

Honest.cash is a paid content publishing platform open to everyone. As you may know, many online platforms and websites help you sell your content to buyers around the world. However, Honest.cash is the first blockchain network that buys content directly from users with Bitcoin. It's a real-time platform where people can exchange skills. To learn more about how it works, you need to go to this platform.

Diaspora Foundation.org

Diaspora is a free software to create a unique community platform that promotes full freedom of work. It is a great online community where people can freely register and start communicating with pioneer buyers from all over the world. Diaspora is simple, but one of the most advanced social networking platforms in the world. It is a blockchain-based network that allows people to be completely anonymous when presenting their skills and expertise to employers.

There are no fixed categories or restrictions on the window that opens to list skills, meaning you can offer any kind of service. DApp stores data in pods on the blockchain network. So you can have full security and authority over your account. You can sell your skills to millions of buyers anonymously at Diasporafoundation.org.

PropsProject

PropsProject is an open source infrastructure that creates a decentralized network of applications and is operated by independent operators. This project aims to empower people who help digital communities to push for improvement. It also creates a bridge between continents to grow together. PropsProject creates digital tokens that can be accessed from any applications, networks, and platforms. The Props token allows people to easily invest and trade in cryptocurrencies. The platform is backed by USV, Venrock, Comcast Ventures, and many others. You can easily connect to any social media platforms like YouTube, Twitch, and Instagram and create Props tokens through your popularity. Easy and simple.

Sapien

Sapien is a Web3 decentralized social network blockchain application, and is one of the most popular in this field. It ensures data sovereignty, meaningful conversations, and economic empowerment. Sapien is a social network that features a cryptocurrency reward system. The main currency here is SPN, which allows rewards to users and is necessary for peer-to-peer communications. Unlike other social networks, Sapien has experienced individuals as members and partners.

With all this data, you can check out and subscribe to the best blockchain decentralized social media platforms that will benefit you the most. Other platforms will come out in the future and maybe some of the ones I wrote above won't last. The blockchain and cryptocurrency field is one of the things to watch for potential opportunities, especially in an era where there is so much suppression of free speech.

Epilogue

Blockchain and cryptocurrencies are undoubtedly the future and will co-exist with the existing financial system. The adoption of cryptocurrencies is growing rapidly around the world by ordinary people who are dissatisfied with the existing banking, government, and financial system and are trying to gain by investing in this promising technology. In general, the winners will be those who can understand this technology to some extent. Of course, there are those who invested early and won a lot of money, as if they had won the lottery. But many of them, who did not understand the basics of finance, investing, and cryptocurrencies, either sold out too early or lost their profits in later investments or something else. That's why understanding the technology is very important, although of course it doesn't guarantee any profit. If one has the knowledge, then one can manage properly and not be influenced by other people's opinions, such as for example "Cryptocurrencies are a bubble" or "Invest in cryptocurrencies and you will be rich," and so on.

Major companies around the world are adopting cryptocurrencies more and more every day, despite their price fluctuations. Some companies invest in cryptocurrencies, while others accept them as a form of payment. Large institutional investors, such as BlackRock, which manages over $10 trillion of its clients' assets, invest in cryptocurrencies. According to speculation and analysis, all institutional investors are expected to invest in cryptocurrencies in the coming years as more and more political reforms come from around the world.

This industry has provided many opportunities over the past 13 years and will continue to provide opportunities in the years to come. In fact, it will never stop because there will always be opportunities. The extent to which someone will exploit the cryptocurrency industry depends first and foremost on their understanding of the industry and then on their choice of how to exploit it. Apart from investing in cryptocurrencies, one can also exploit it in various other ways, as well as the internet technology we have so far. It could create new jobs, contribute to the development of this technology in various ways, and provide solutions in this area in any way it can.

In this book, I have presented a guide to gain a basic understanding of this revolutionary technology through its various pieces, such as DeFi, NFTs, wallets, exchanges, and more. It is a complete guide to the basic and essential knowledge of this technology. On my YouTube channel, at the time of writing, I have already uploaded over 4000 videos on cryptocurrencies, averaging 10 minutes each. They have been viewed by over 1000,000+ people in Greece, Cyprus and all over the world and have had over 13 million views so far.

The information shared in this book is based on current technological development. In the future, many things will change because this technology is constantly changing and improving. I believe that anyone who wants to get serious about cryptocurrencies should broaden their knowledge and constantly monitor developments in the industry. Things that are in place now may be different in a year due to changes and upgrades in technology or projects or due to political reforms. But, anyone who has a good and basic knowledge of this industry will be able to monitor and understand future changes.

Cryptocurrencies give people the freedom and independence they would like to have for the toil and sweat of their lives – their money and their assets. That effort is increasingly being lost as there are increasingly concerted efforts to gain total control by governments, the banking system, and big companies – especially the tech ones. One means of exercising this control is the CBDC (Central Bank Digital Currency), which is digital money for the dollar, the euro, and other countries' currencies. With this, they can control people's money, as we have seen done in science fiction movies. Some countries have already piloted it. In 2023, the US will also pilot the digital dollar and then Europe will follow.

CBDCs and cryptocurrencies are each other's worst enemy. One (CBDC) aims for absolute control from a central point – governments and banking systems, while the other (cryptocurrencies) provides freedom of movement, ownership, and independence from the existing system, autonomously from a decentralized system. In the past and until recently, efforts were made by the banking system and various governments to fight cryptocurrencies. To some extent, it is still going on, but less and less, because they can no longer oppose the people, because they know they will lose voters and the people will revolt. Now we see politicians supporting cryptocurrencies more and more, and promising their voters that they will be cryptocurrency-friendly if they are elected. I personally believe that CBDC and cryptocurrencies will co-exist.

In the eyes of many people, cryptocurrencies and CBDCs are seen as the "good" and the "bad." In my opinion, it is worth supporting this technology – cryptocurrencies – for the purpose it has, not necessarily to make an investment, as there are other ways to support it. Of course, the fact that it is worth supporting should not be taken as an encouragement to invest.

In conclusion, cryptocurrencies are an exciting new technological development that has the potential to revolutionize the way we interact with the digital world. With their unique features and advantages, they are poised to become a major force in the global economy. As more people begin to recognize their potential, we are likely to see even greater adoption of this innovative technology, which is constantly evolving. That's why I believe that the winner in the end will be the one who understands more and more about cryptocurrencies or the financial situation in general!

Glossary

aBFT (Asynchronous Byzantine Fault Tolerant)

It is a consensus protocol. Here, the word "Byzantine" has the meaning of "complex system."

Airdrop

A marketing campaign that distributes a specific cryptocurrency or token to an audience.

Altcoin

As Bitcoin was the first cryptocurrency that captured the imagination of the world, all other currencies were then called "altcoins," as in "alternative currencies."

Annual Percentage Rate (APR)

The amount of interest a borrower must pay each year is known as the annual percentage rate (APR). The annual percentage rate (APR) is determined by multiplying the periodic rate by the number of periods in a year in which the periodic rate is used.

Annual Percentage Yield (APY)

Annual Percentage Yield (APY) is the percentage of return earned over the course of a year from a particular investment. APY includes subsidiary interest, which is calculated on a regular basis and applied to the amount.

API (Application Programming Interface)

It is software that provides a way for two or more computer programs to communicate with each other. It provides a user interface that connects two or more programs by performing tasks in them. APIs define how these programs interact with each other, such as what data to use and what actions to take.

Arbitrage

Arbitrage is the practice of quickly buying and selling the same asset in different Marketplaces to take advantage of price differences between the Marketplaces.

Bear

Someone who believes that prices in a given market will fall for a long time. Such a person may be referred to as "bearish."

Bear Market

When asset prices in a market fall by 20% or more from recent highs, it is called a bear market. As a result, investor confidence is low and the economy and market become pessimistic.

Bear Trap

An attempt to manipulate the price of a particular cryptocurrency based on the coordinated activity of a group of traders.

BEP2

The BEP2 token standard is the first native token standard for the Binance chain and is limited to the Binance ecosystem.

BFT (Byzantine Fault Tolerant)

It is a consensus protocol, with the word "Byzantine" here meaning "complex system."

Big Tech

The four or five largest technology companies in the United States. Currently they are Meta (Facebook), Apple, Alphabet (Google), Amazon, and Microsoft. They are referred to as "Big Tech" because they enjoy the largest shares in their respective industries.

Bit

The bit is a basic unit of information in computers.

Bitcoin ATM (BTM)

An automated teller machine (ATM or cash point) that allows the user to buy and sell Bitcoins.

Block

A record containing information about transactions completed during a given period of time. Blocks are the constituent parts of a blockchain.

Blockchain

A distributed ledger system. A sequence (chain) of blocks, or units of digital information, stored sequentially in a public database. It is the basis for cryptocurrencies.

BSC (Binance Smart Chain)

Binance Smart Chain is an innovative solution for introducing interoperability and programming to the Binance Chain.

Bubble

When an asset trades at a price that exceeds the intrinsic value of that asset.

Bull

A person who is optimistic and certain that market prices will rise. This person is also known as "bullish."

Bull Market

A Bull Market in cryptocurrencies and stock markets refers to a period in which asset prices rise too much. These markets act as a source of motivation for both investors and buyers. It is not a permanent situation, although it can remain for months or even years.

Bull Run

An upward trend (also known as an uptrend). It is a period of time in the financial market during which the values of certain assets are continuously increasing.

Bull Trap

The situation where an asset that is steadily declining appears to reverse and go up, but soon resumes its downward trend. It acts as a trap for some investors, hence its name.

Burn/Burned/Burning

Cryptocurrency tokens or coins are considered "burned" when they have been deliberately and permanently removed from circulation.

Buy The (Fucking) Dip (BTD/BTFD)

An enthusiastic exclamation from supporters of a cryptocurrency to buy when prices are at a low point.

Central Bank

In modern economies, the central bank is responsible for the formulation and transmission of monetary policy, as well as for the regulation of member banks.

Central Bank Digital Currency

CBDCs are digital currencies issued by a central bank, whose status as legal tender depends on legislation.

Centralized

A centralized organizational structure is one in which a single node or a small number of nodes have control of an entire network.

Centralized exchanges (CEX)

A type of cryptocurrency exchanges that are operated by a company that holds them in a centralized manner.

Coin

A coin may refer to a cryptocurrency that can operate independently or to a single unit of such cryptocurrency.

Cold Storage

Store cryptocurrency offline. Usually includes software for wallets but is offline and without hardware, USBs, CDs, offline computers, or paper wallets.

Cold Wallet

A cryptocurrency wallet that is in cold storage, i.e. not connected to the internet.

Contract
In traditional finance, a contract is a binding agreement between two parties. In cryptocurrencies, smart contracts perform functions on the blockchain.

Crowdfunding
Crowdfunding enables fundraisers to raise money from large numbers of people through a variety of different platforms.

Cryptoasset
Any digital asset that uses cryptographic technologies to maintain its function as a currency or decentralized application.

Cryptocurrency
Digital currencies that use cryptographic technologies to ensure their operation.
Cryptocurrency Money Laundering
A method used by criminals to monetize and encapsulate funds by changing a fiat currency into digital currency and then routing it through multiple routes. It is an attempt to make the authorities lose track when they are looking for the money.

Currency
Currency is a medium of exchange that determines value.

DAO (Decentralized Autonomous Organization)
In general terms, DAOs are member-owned communities without centralized leadership. A DAO is based and governed by a set of computer-defined rules and blockchain-based smart contracts. Another name for DAO is DAC (Decentralized Autonomous Corporation).

Day Trading

Day Trading is the practice of frequently buying and selling assets in order to make a profit from the changes in their price that occur during the day.

Decentralized

Decentralization refers to the property of a system in which nodes work together in a distributed way to achieve a common goal.

Decentralized API (dAPI)

API services, which are inherently interoperable with blockchain technology, are known as decentralized application programming interfaces (dAPIs).

Decentralized Application (DApp)

A type of application that runs autonomously on a decentralized network. Like traditional applications, DApps provide some function or utility to their users. However, unlike traditional applications, DApps run without human intervention and are not owned by any entity.

Decentralized Currency

Decentralized Currency refers to methods of transferring wealth without banks or methods of owning any other commodity without the need for a third party or intermediary.

Decentralized Exchange (DEX)

A peer-to-peer exchange that allows users to trade cryptocurrencies without the need for an intermediary.

Deep Web

The "deep web" is the part of the internet that is hidden from normal search engines.

DeFi (Decentralized Finance)
Decentralized Finance is financing that offers financial instruments without relying on intermediaries (brokerages, exchanges, or banks) using smart contracts on blockchain.

Diamond Hands
Diamond Hands is a popular term on social media platforms. It refers to people who hold on to their coins even if their portfolio drops in value by more than 20%.

Digital Currency
A currency that exists only in digital form, unlike traditional physical currencies.

Digital Dollar
The term "Digital Dollar" refers to a possible digital currency issued by the US Central Bank (CBDC).

Dip
A dip is when markets experience a short or prolonged fall – a recession.

Discord
Discord is a VoIP (Voice over IP or internet telephony) platform where messaging and digital sharing takes place. It is designed for community building. Users can communicate with voice calls, video calls, text messages, multimedia, and files in private conversations or in communities.

Diversification
Diversification is a risk management strategy that combines a wide variety of investments in a portfolio.

Dump

A sudden sell-off of digital assets.

Dumping

A collective sell-off in the market, which occurs when large quantities of a particular cryptocurrency are sold in a short period of time.

ERC-20

Its name stands for Ethereum Request for Comments 20. It is a token designed and used exclusively on the Ethereum platform.

Ether

The payment method, the currency, used in the operation of the Ethereum platform.

Exchange

Business that allows customers to exchange cryptocurrencies for fiat money or other cryptocurrencies.

Fan Token

A fan token is a cryptocurrency issued by a specific sports team. It allows its holders to participate in inter-governmental activities and achieve exclusive rewards and discounts.

Farming (or Yield Farming)

It involves lending or staking cryptocurrencies in exchange for interest and other rewards.

Fiat (currency)

Fiat currency is "legal tender" that derives its value from the government that issues it, not from a physical good or commodity. It is backed by a central government, such as the Federal Reserve, and with its own banking system. It may be in the form of physical cash or it may be represented electronically, such as by bank credit.

Flash Loans

Contingency loans are a type of unsecured lending used in decentralized finance (DeFi).

FOMO

An acronym meaning "Fear of Missing Out."

GameFi

Better known as play 2 earn (P2E), is a rather new term in both the gaming and cryptocurrency industry. It refers to games designed with financial aspects of blockchain and cryptocurrencies, enabling players to exert full control over their in-game assets in order to generate revenue.

Gas

A term used on the Ethereum platform that refers to a unit of measurement of the computational effort required to conduct transactions or smart contracts or to initiate DApps on the Ethereum network. It is the "fuel" of the Ethereum network.

Gas limit

A term used on the Ethereum platform that refers to the maximum amount of gas a user is willing to spend in a transaction.

Gas price / Gas fees

A term used on the Ethereum platform that refers to the price a user is going to pay for a transaction.

Halving

An event in which the total rewards per confirmed block are halved.

Hard Cap

The hard cap is the absolute maximum bid of a digital item.

Hard Fork

It is related to blockchain technology. It is a radical change in a network's protocol that makes all previously invalid blocks and transactions valid, or vice versa. A hard fork requires all nodes or users to upgrade to the latest version of the protocol software.

Hardware Wallet

A Hardware wallet is a cryptocurrency wallet that usually looks like a USB stick.
Hash

It is used for fragmentation. It is the result of a mathematical hash function (algorithm) that maps key names to integer numbers. The integers that result from the function are the hash values, i.e. the hash.

HODL

A type of passive investment strategy where an investment is held for a long period of time, regardless of any changes in price or markets. The term originally became famous due to a typo made on a Bitcoin forum. The term is now commonly extended to mean "Hold On for Dear Life."

Hot Storage

The electronic storage of private keys, that allows faster access to cryptocurrencies.

Hot Wallet

A cryptocurrency wallet that is connected to the Internet for cryptographic data storage, as opposed to an offline, cold wallet with cold storage.

Initial Coin Offering (ICO)

An ICO is a type of public financing or public sale that uses cryptocurrencies as a means of raising capital for early-stage companies.

Initial Dex Offering (IDO)

It is an alternative to an Initial Coin Offering (ICO) that takes place on a Decentralized Exchange (Dex).

Initial Public Offering (IPO)

It is the process by which a company offers shares for purchase on the stock exchange for the first time.

Internet of Things (IoT)

The Internet of Things is the communication network of a multitude of devices, home appliances, cars, and any object that incorporates electronic media, software, sensors, and network connectivity to allow connection and exchange of data.

Know Your Customer (KYC)

These are checks that cryptocurrency exchanges and trading platforms must complete to verify the identity of their customers.

Layer 2
It is the name given to a scaling solution that enables high transaction performance while fully inheriting the security of the underlying blockchain on which it is built.

Ledger
A file containing financial transactions, cannot be changed, and only new transactions are added to it.

Leverage
Money that a trader borrows from a brokerage, allowing him to gain much more exposure to a position than his own capital allows.

Lightning Network
A layer 2 protocol designed to solve Bitcoin's scalability problem by allowing faster transaction processing.

Liquidity
How easily a cryptocurrency can be bought and sold without affecting the overall market price.

Liquidity Pool
Liquidity Pools are cryptocurrency assets held to facilitate the trading of trading pairs on decentralized exchanges.
Liquidity Provider Token (LP token)
Liquidity Provider tokens or LP tokens are tokens given to liquidity providers on a decentralized exchange (DEX), executed using an Automated Market Maker (AMM) protocol (a system that provides liquidity to the exchange on which it operates through automated transactions).

Long

A situation where you buy a cryptocurrency with the expectation of selling it later at a higher price to make a profit.

Mainnet

An independent blockchain running its own network with its own technology and protocol.

Margin Trading

A practice where a trader uses borrowed funds from a broker to trade a cryptocurrency.

Market Capitalisation – Market Cap/MCAP

Total capitalization of the price of a cryptocurrency. It is one of the ways of ranking the relative size of a cryptocurrency. For a cryptocurrency like Bitcoin, the market capitalization is the total value of all the coins that have been mined. It is calculated by multiplying the number of coins in circulation by the current market price of the coin.

Memecoin

Memecoins are cryptocurrencies that are created as a joke and claim to offer huge profits to holders.

Meta (Meta Platforms Inc.)

Multinational technology group in the USA. It controls Facebook, Instagram, and WhatsApp, among other products and services.

MetaMask

An online digital wallet that allows users to manage, transfer, and receive Ethereum by acting as an extension to a regular browser.

Metaverse

A metaverse is a digital universe that contains all aspects of the real world, such as interactions and economies, in real time. It offers a unique experience to end users.

Node

The most basic blockchain infrastructure unit that stores data.

Non-fungible token (NFT)

Non-fungible tokens (NFTs) are encrypted elements that do not have the property of being exchangeable. They can be associated either with any digital artwork file, such as photographs, video, audio, and other types of multimedia, or with a digital representation of a physical object.

Option

It is a contract that gives the buyer the right – but not the obligation – to buy or sell the underlying asset at a certain price on or before a certain date.

Peer-to-peer (P2P)

Decentralized interactions between parties in a distributed network, task separation, or peer-to-peer workload.

Perpetual swaps trading

In finance, a perpetual futures contract, also known as a perpetual swap, is an agreement to buy or sell an asset at an unspecified point in the future.

Play-to-Earn (Play2Earn)

The play-to-earn business model supports the concept of an open economy and gives financial rewards to players who add value to its metaverse.

Proof-of-Coverage (PoC)

It is an algorithm that attempts to verify, on a continuous basis, that hotspots honestly represent their location and the wireless network coverage they create from that location. It is used by the Helium blockchain.

Proof-of-History (PoH)

It is an algorithm that plays an important role in Solana's Proof of Stake (PoS) consensus mechanism. It has the concept of proving that something happened before or after a known event, rather than relying on a timestamp.

Proof-of-Stake (PoS)

A blockchain consensus mechanism, created as an alternative to the Proof of Work (PoW), that maintains the integrity of the blockchain. It works by selecting users who validate transactions on the chain according to the amount of their holdings in the associated cryptocurrency.

Proof-of-Work (PoW)

A blockchain consensus mechanism that involves solving computationally intensive puzzles to validate transactions and create new blocks.

Pump and Dump (P&D).

A form of fraud that involves artificially inflating the price of a cryptocurrency with false and misleading positive statements.

Ransomware

Ransomware is a type of malware used by hackers to steal or encrypt their victims' files and extort them for ransom in exchange for decrypting or restoring files.

Regulation

It is when something is controlled or regulated by a certain set of rules.

Roadmap

It is a high-level visual summary that helps map the vision as well as the direction of a particular product.

ROI

Abbreviation of the term "Return on Investment." It is the ratio between net profit (or loss) and investment cost.

Rug Pull

Rug Pull is a type of scam where developers abandon a project, take their investors' money and disappear.

S&P 500 (Standard and Poor's 500)

The Standard and Poor's 500, also known as the S&P 500, is a stock market index that represents a list of the 500 largest companies located in the United States and their market performance.

Satoshi (SATS)

The smallest Bitcoin unit with a value of 0.00000001 BTC.

Satoshi Nakamoto

The individual or group of individuals who created Bitcoin.

Security

The term "securities" refers to an exchangeable and negotiable financial instrument that carries some kind of monetary value.

Security Token

A security token is essentially a digital form of traditional securities.

Shitcoin

A coin with no obvious potential value or use.

Short

A trading technique in which a trader borrows an asset to sell it immediately and get the money, with the expectation that the price will fall. If the price does fall, the short trader will then buy the asset at that low price. He then returns the asset to the lender to close his loan, and the difference between the price he sold it at (high) and the price he bought it at (low) gives him the profit.

Silk Road

An online black market that existed on the dark web, now shut down by the FBI.

Smart Contracts

Smart contracts, in fact, are not really about contracts. They are programs stored on the blockchain along with information about coins, tokens, and wallets. They are the key to developing decentralized applications based on cryptocurrencies.

Soft Fork

A "soft fork" is a change to the protocol, which is still compatible with previous system rules. It only adds whatever new thing is needed to the new currency or token.

Spot

A contract or transaction to buy or sell cryptocurrency for immediate settlement or payment and delivery of the cryptocurrency to the market.

Spot Market

A public market in which cryptocurrencies are traded for direct settlement. It is in contrast to a futures market, in which settlement is due at a later date.

Spot Trading

Spot trading involves the direct exchange of a financial instrument at the current price.

Stablecoin

It is a cryptocurrency whose value is linked to the value of another currency, commodity, or financial instrument. Stablecoin aims to provide an alternative to the high volatility of the most popular cryptocurrencies, including Bitcoin (BTC). Therefore, it is a cryptocurrency with extremely low volatility. Examples of stablecoins include cryptocurrencies connected to gold or cryptocurrencies connected to fiat.

Staking

Participation in a Proof of Stake (PoS) system that serves for validation on the blockchain. Depending on the amount of tokens you have, you can validate transactions to receive rewards.

Staking Pool

Staking Pool allows users to combine their resources to increase their chances of earning rewards. This mechanism provides greater staking power to the network for verifying and validating new blocks.

Taproot

Taproot is an implementation of a soft fork for Bitcoin, intended both to improve privacy and to improve other aspects associated with more complex transactions.

Testnet

An alternative blockchain used by developers for testing.

Token

A digital unit designed with utility in mind and can be programmed. It has its own code, which is related to an existing chain. These digital modules facilitate the creation of decentralized applications. They provide access to and are used in the financial systems of cryptocurrencies.

Total Supply

The total number of coins that currently exist, minus any coins that are confirmed to have been burned.

Total Value Locked (TVL)

The total locked value represents the number of assets currently being staked on a particular protocol.

Trade Volume

The amount of cryptocurrency traded in the last 24 hours.

Trading Bot

A cryptocurrency trading bot is essentially a program designed to automate the trading of cryptocurrency assets on behalf of the trader.

Volume

How many cryptocurrencies have been traded in a specified period, such as in the last 24 hours.

Web 1.0

Web 1.0 is a term often used to describe the early version of the internet.

Web 2.0

Web 2.0 describes the current state of the web, which supports more user-generated content and stability for front-end users than its predecessor, Web 1.0.

Web 3.0 or Web3

Web 3.0 is the third generation of the technological evolution of the Internet. It is an idea for a new iteration of the World Wide Web, incorporating concepts such as decentralization, blockchain technologies, and a token-based economy.

Wei

The smallest fraction of an Ether, with each Ether being 1000000000000000000000 Wei.

Whale

A term used to describe investors who have unusually large amounts of cryptocurrency, especially those with enough capital to manipulate the market.

Whitepaper

A document released by a cryptocurrency project that gives investors technical information about its concept and a roadmap of how it plans to grow and succeed.

Yield Farming

Lending or staking cryptocurrencies in exchange for interest and other rewards.

Bibliography – References

This book contains information and data, as well as definitions of terms taken from the following sources:

wikipedia.com

wiktionary.org

investopedia.com

coinmarketcap.com

binance.com

crypto.com

forbes.com

coindesk.com

Information, data, terms, and definitions have also been taken from the respective platforms, exchanges, or applications mentioned in the book.

Scan the QR code or visit *andreouuniversity.com*

Giannis Andreou YouTube Channel

Giannis Andreou Instagram

Giannis Andreou Twitter